Classic Dormobile Camper Vans

A Guide to the Camper Vans of Martin Walter and Dormobile

Classic Dormobile Camper Vans

A Guide to the Camper Vans of Martin Walter and Dormobile

Martin Watts

The Crowood Press

First published in 2009 by
The Crowood Press Ltd
Ramsbury, Marlborough
Wiltshire SN8 2HR

www.crowood.com

British Library Cataloguing-in-Publication Data
A catalogue record for this book is available from the British Library.

ISBN 978 1 84797 083 1

Typeset and designed by D & N Publishing
Lambourn Woodlands, Hungerford, Berkshire.

Printed and bound in Malaysia by Times Offset (M) Sdn. Bhd.

contents

dedication

This book is dedicated to my wife Dilys and my two sons Tom and Austin.

acknowledgements

This book has been compiled with the help and assistance of many people from the world of motorcaravanning in the United Kingdom. In particular, I thank the family of the late John Hunt for allowing me to use many photographs from his personal collection. In addition, I would like to record my thanks to all the owners of period and classic campers who have assisted me with information, and allowed me to photograph their beloved vehicles.

A special word of thanks is due to all the past authors who have so skilfully recorded the models, events, price guides and the definitive information so vital in both the research and the preparation of this book.

Most of the photographs and press pictures used in this book came from the archive of the author. The following people kindly supplied other photographs used: Melanie Chalk and Bob Brisley (Folkestone Camera Club), Alan Kirtley, Tony Fernley, Nick Stoton, Rosie Taylor, Bob Darling, Alan and Cath Houchen, the Standard Motor Club, Bill Bradford-TLR Land Rover Parts, of Pittsburg, Tennessee, Steve Cooper, Dave Hodgson, Jean Beesley, Patrick Osborne, Robin Phillips, Scott and Bex, Mike Scott, Benson Langley and Matt Traxton.

I should also thank any owner, not mentioned above, who has given me photographs to use as I saw fit. Over the years many owners have given me valuable archive material in the form of books, sales brochures, photographs, price guides and newspaper cuttings, again to use as I wished. Although I have never recorded these people by name (there were quite simply far too many) they will, of course, be well aware of who they are when reading this acknowledgement. Their kindness has allowed me to put together a valuable archive of Martin Walter/Dormobile material from years gone by; my sincere thanks to them all.

It would be remiss of me not to mention the former employees of Martin Walter Ltd/Dormobile Ltd who worked for the company over the course of many years. They all played a part (no matter how large or small) in creating a slice of motoring history. It is a testament to the design and build quality at the company that so many vehicles produced at the several Folkestone sites have survived to this day in the hands of dedicated vehicle enthusiasts throughout the world.

Some words, model names and designations are trademarked and are the property of the trademark owners. They have been used for identification purposes only and this is not an official publication.

While every effort has been made to ensure the accuracy of all material, the author and publisher cannot accept liability for any loss resulting from any error, misstatement, inaccuracy or omission contained herein. The author welcomes any corrections or additional information.

introduction

Few motor vehicles have ever given their brand name to the English language, only two spring immediately to mind, the 'Mini' and the 'Dormobile'. When Richard Lyne-Smith, a director of the Martin Walter Company, devised the term Dormobile for their utility vehicles, he could not have envisaged that it would still be in use by people in the United Kingdom some fifty years later. The concept was quite brilliant; drawing upon his knowledge of Latin, he took 'dorm' from *dormire*, to sleep, and added to it 'mobile' to make it perfectly obvious that the vehicle was a sleeping-mobile. The rest, as they say, is history, but a history never before laid down in such a concise manner.

There was rivalry in Europe between the English and the Germans in the race to claim first place in the development of the motor car and of the motor caravan. Carl Benz managed to beat the Englishman Charles Santler to claim victory in developing the first motor car, and the Germans won once again with their motor caravan conversion on the Volkswagen van. The matter of motor car precedence is still debated as Benz and Santler did work on their separate designs at the same time and did communicate with each other. The motor caravan issue is clearer cut; legend has it that an English army officer, on seeing the (then) new Volkswagen van, commissioned Westfalia to add some suitable bedding, cupboards and cooking facilities, from which the iconic VW camper van evolved.

If only Martin Walter Ltd had added some simple 'living' units to their Utilicon (general utility) vehicles during the 1940s they could have laid claim to producing the first European camper van. Martin Walter had been producing a large number of converted personnel vehicles during the Second World War for the armed services, and the Royal Navy in particular. These had contained the forerunner of the Dormatic seating later designed for the Dormobile Caravan. These seats could be altered by using a variety of springs and sliding mechanisms to form lay-flat seats on which to sleep; but the vehicles fell short of being fully-fitted camper vans due to the lack of any cooking and washing facilities. With some simple additions, Martin Walter could have been producing camper vans some ten years before the first Volkswagen examples appeared.

With regard to the period from 1952 through to the appearance of the first (fully fitted) Dormobile Caravan in 1957, there are probably more questions than answers concerning camper van development in the United Kingdom. The Bedford CA had been introduced; it was immediately popular as a light commercial van, cute to look at (just like the early VW van) and with a split front windscreen, again like the VW. The Bedford also had far more usable interior space for conversion to a camper van due to the location of the Vauxhall engine at the front. Martin Walter Ltd had already fitted their Dormatic seating in the vehicle, enabling people to sleep in it, which raises the obvious question: why did the company

This very early picture shows some of the staff at Martin Walter Ltd building a wooden-framed car in the 1920s. Note the lack of windows in the building, with only a rooflight panel allowing light to filter through over the car assembly area. These are probably the premises located on Tontine Street, Folkestone.

not go the extra mile and build a camper van from 1952? Sadly, we shall never know the answer, as such important decisions would have been taken by senior company directors, and none of them survive from that period. We are left to assume that they felt that a market for such fully-fitted vehicles did not exist in the United Kingdom at that time.

As it was, Peter Pitt of London produced the first fully-fitted camper van introduced in the United Kingdom. Pitt's 'open plan' layout based on a VW van was extremely ingenious, allowing the user to move furniture around within the vehicle to create more than one seating/sleeping configuration. The success of this obviously spurred Martin Walter into action since shortly after they released their own version, the Dormobile Caravan, based on the Bedford CA. This time it was fully-fitted

as a camper van, with cupboards, cooker and sink, on-board water containers and a rising roof.

It is well to remember that in the mid-1950s camper vans and larger, factory-built motorhomes simply did not exist, and the likes of Peter Pitt, Martin Walter Ltd and Maurice Calthorpe were the pioneers of the motor caravan industry in the United Kingdom. Others would quickly follow, such as Jack White (Devon), Bluebird and Central Garage, who would all unveil their own motor caravan creations within a couple of years of each other. If ever there were an admirable product released at the ideal point in time, then the Dormobile Caravan was it. The Dormobile Caravan was the most affordable of the new style camper vans coming on to the market, it was also simple in its design and made use of a popular, light, com-

mercial van of the period, the Bedford CA. It was the perfect recipe for retail success in a growing leisure market, and, as the 1950s and 1960s developed, the Dormobile camper would sell in huge numbers, becoming an extremely common sight on the British roads.

This book will chart the history of the Martin Walter Company from the golden age of coachbuilt bodies on luxury cars, to the utility vehicles constructed on vans. But the main focus will be the motor caravans produced at the famous Folkestone factory in Kent in England. Every camper van model made by the company will be featured, some of which are very familiar and instantly recognizable, others less so. It was my intention when writing this book to record a section of British motoring history never before described, and certainly long overdue.

Looking down on the Tile Kiln Lane site today.

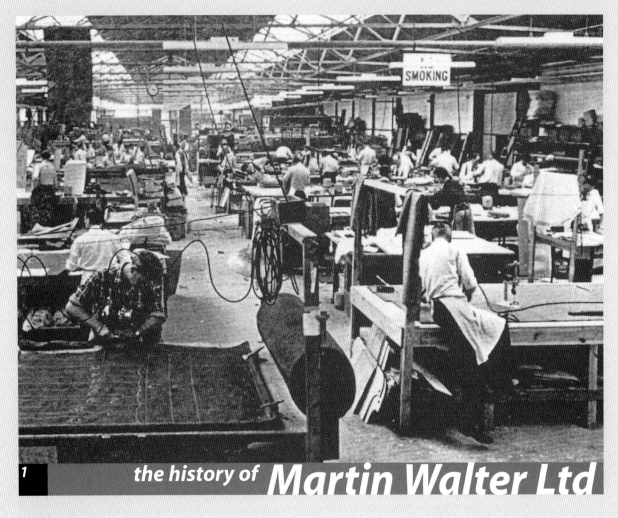

Inside the busy 'Trim Shop' at Martin Walter. A busy workforce prepares materials for seats, headlining, door cards and many more applications.

1 the history of *Martin Walter Ltd*

The Martin Walter story began in 1773 when the Walter family first set up a saddle and harness business in Southgate, in north London. John Walter (presumably a descendant of Martin) moved to Folkestone many years later, leaving behind the established family business. John set up as a saddle and harness maker in the town and married a local girl Mabel Apps. He placed an advertisement in a local newspaper around 1890, seeking the services of an apprentice. The pay was set at three shillings a week rising to nine shillings after seven years. The holiday entitlement for the successful applicant was two days per year, Christmas day and Good Friday. The move to Folkestone was to prove profitable for John as the Shorncliffe army camp (based in Folkestone) was full of mounted regiments, all, of course, requiring repairs to saddles and harnesses. In 1911, with his wife Mabel and brother-in-law Spencer Apps, John formed a limited company Martin Walter Ltd and Spencer became the

managing director. With the help of just one assistant they opened a showroom in Sandgate Road, Folkestone. The new company became a success and soon afterwards they took over the local coach-maker Hill & Co. Apps first took up motoring in the early part of the twentieth century and by 1912 had opened a car showroom. From this point Martin Walter Ltd would build both motor car bodies and horse carriages.

Spencer Apps did not succumb to the idea of being an 'exclusive' franchise, opting instead to sell a variety of marques; these included Austin, Aston Martin, Daimler, Hudson, Hillman, Lagonda, MG, Sunbeam and Vauxhall. Apps would not confine his chassis buying to British marques, sometimes making purchases from abroad such as the Delage. The clientele for these motor cars was drawn initially from the Kent and East Sussex area. In 1921 the company exhibited its products at Olympia for the first time, thus drawing in a far bigger audience for their coach-building skills. By

this time, the original premises in Tontine Street, Folkestone were already being outgrown and in the late 1920s they moved to a more suitable location in Cheriton Road. Martin Walter Ltd were by this time advertising themselves as 'exhibition coachbuilders' and were firmly established as one of the leaders in their field in the British motor industry.

Martin Walter's first 'show' cars were examples of the 12/20HP Bianchi and the 14/20HP Panhard. These were all-weather bodies featuring adjustable front seats, controllable side windows and custom tool kits. Later the company would produce passenger-carrying cabriolets, complete with 'dickey' seats. Examples included the DI Delage, Roesch Talbot and LM-type Vauxhall. In fact, the Vauxhall model (complete with golf club locker) sold for £720, which was £25 more than the version built by Grosvenor, Vauxhall's own coachbuilder. Martin Walter were also producing sporting bodies mounted on the Bentley chassis, and some limousines built

Typical of the coachwork carried out by Martin Walter during the 1920s and the 1930s, this is a 1926 Bentley 3-litre mounted on a 'Red Label' chassis, in the sporting style. The fish-shaped aerofoil running board was quite fashionable during this period.

on the Daimler, the Delage and the Hispano-Suiza. From 1927 cellulose paint and the fabric system of construction had been introduced at the factory, and in 1928 the Martin Walter display at Olympia included a 6½-litre Bentley limousine with a price tag of £2,150. This was indeed the era of opulent coachwork and in 1929 the company built the Speed Six Folkestone sports saloon, designed to accommodate four people and featuring a shallow screen and high waistline. This model also incorporated luncheon and wine cabinets.

By this period the body works at Cheriton Road were employing around sixty people, and a customer's order could be built from scratch within three months, with all designs worked out on a blackboard in the factory. As the great economic depression of the period struck, Martin Walter did branch out into semi-series coachwork on many popular chassis, though they continued to receive the more 'elite' orders throughout. Among these was a stylish design based on the 20-25 Rolls-Royce

chassis and supplied to Lord Carnarvon in 1932. Regular factory styles at this time included the Romney coupé, the Denton, and the Cheriton four-door saloon with fabric top and integral trunk. Their full programme for 1932 included closer links with Vauxhall, and such Vauxhall models were invoiced through the manufacturer and sold in Vauxhall retail outlets; this no doubt paved the way for the close bond between Martin Walter Ltd and Vauxhall during the 1950s.

In 1933 the first of the Wingham bodies appeared, revered to this day as one of the all-time great Martin Walter car models (though the 'Wingham' style was not exclusive to Martin Walter). Their factory Wingham became so successful that a new company Wingham Martin Walter Ltd was formed in order to build these four-door cabriolets at a factory at Capel, between Folkestone and Dover. These bespoke bodies were now being built at the rate of 250 units a year at the Capel factory. At the peak of Wingham production the bodies were offered on three different chassis, including the

Vauxhall Fourteen at £295 and the Daimler light-twenty at £750. It was all to change by 1937, since by this time Hillman had given up on the large car market, Daimler were now buying cabriolets from Salmons and Vauxhall were committed to chassis-less construction techniques. But the driving force behind the company, Spencer Apps, had pre-empted this situation and in 1935 had registered a new design, the 'Utilicon'. This was an all-steel station wagon, a type of motor vehicle not seen in the United Kingdom before, and Apps had quite possibly taken his idea from the successful Ford half-timbered estate car. But, as a commercial vehicle, the new Martin Walter Utilicon would be subject to a 30mph speed restriction, in line with British motoring law. The Utilicon made its debut on the Fordson 8/10cwt, forward-control chassis. It would be this model that became the standard naval and civil defence passenger transport during the Second World War, although some other versions were produced on the Morris and Bedford. When it came to the war effort, Martin Walter were not only producing the Utilicon vehicle, but they also moved around 150 tons of equipment to a factory in Thames Ditton in order to produce shells and missiles.

During the war years another local Kent company, Tapley Motors, forged close links with Martin Walter Ltd to produce several utility vehicles for the armed forces. In 1946 Tapley Motors was taken over by Martin Walter, and Don Tapley became a finance director, and later company chairman of Martin Walter. He remained in this position until Martin Walter was acquired by Charringtons in the 1960s. Tapley's son David Tapley had also joined Martin Walter and became heavily involved in the development of the Dormobile motor caravans.

After the war the company switched its production focus from hand-built, luxury motor cars to light commercial models. This type/style of vehicle was much in vogue in Britain as the country recovered from the ravages of war and began a prolonged period of rebuilding.

In 1952 Vauxhall Motors launched the Bedford CA van, a light commercial built by using mechanical elements from the Vauxhall Wyvern (later Victor) car. A new chapter in British motoring history was about to commence as Vauxhall and

This 'Double-Six' Daimler dates from 1932 and clearly illustrates the type of bespoke body that was gaining in popularity.

ABOVE: The idea of a 'Utilicon' van was devised by Spencer Apps in 1935. This consisted of a basic 10cwt van converted to carry both goods and people. During the Second World War the Royal Navy gave this van the nickname 'Tilly'. It was put to use on board large ships and in naval dockyards.

RIGHT: The 'Wingham' cabriolet was not exclusive to Martin Walter Ltd, but they certainly produced some of the best examples. This was a four-door cabriolet with folding hood available on such base vehicles as the Lanchester, Vauxhall and Hillman. This advertisement dates from October 1935.

ABOVE: The driving force behind the Martin Walter empire for many years was this man, H. Spencer Apps. He fulfilled a variety of roles within the company, including that of chairman.

Martin Walter entered into one of the greatest motoring partnerships. Upon the Bedford CA base Martin Walter would build just about every conceivable type of vehicle, from the Utilibus to the Workobus, pick-up trucks, mobile shops and, from the mid-1950s, the Dormobile Caravan. In 1955 just less than 9 acres (3.6ha) of land was purchased at Tile Kiln Lane, and a factory in excess of 140,000sq ft (13,000sq m) was built, especially for the production of the Bedford CA models. Three men were the driving force behind the success of the Martin Walter Company from this time: Spencer Apps, the director Richard Lyne-Smith and the designer Cecil Carte. Lyne-Smith is held to have 'invented' the name Dormobile, while Carte was the original designer of the Dormobile Bedford Caravan and is credited with the design of the famous candy-stripe rising roof. Between them they would create a British motoring icon, recognizable everywhere. The Bedford Caravan became the biggest selling vehicle of its

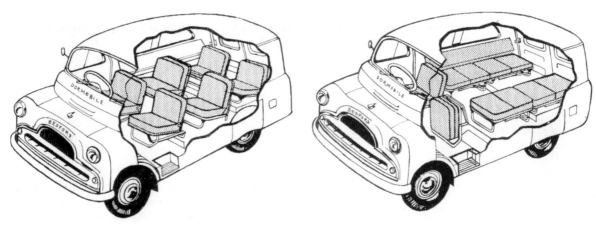

Martin Walter first unveiled the 'Dormobile' in 1952, based on the Bedford CA – a versatile design, which allowed for the carrying of both goods and passengers, with the added benefit that the seats could be arranged for sleeping when required. The diagram on the left illustrates the seats arranged for travelling, while the picture on the right clearly shows the seats transformed into beds.

type in a short period of time, helped by the fact that it was the most affordable camper van in the United Kingdom.

By 1960 the company had produced the ten-thousandth Bedford CA conversion (in all forms, camper and utility), and new base vehicles were arriving by rail at the Folkestone factory aboard the Dormobile Special steam train. By now the company had added the Ford Thames 400E, the Standard Atlas and the BMC J2 to its camper van model line-up. As the new decade began, the Rootes Commer, the BMC J4 and the Land Rover were given as base-vehicle options, though the Bedford CA would remain the principal model, and by this time their Dormobile camper vans accounted for over 80 per cent of the factory output.

Throughout the 1960s the company remained at the forefront of camper van production in the country, with the

Dormobile conversion of the Bedford CA continuing to sell in huge numbers. By 1964 Martin Walter Ltd were once again breaking new ground with the introduction of their innovative Debonair motor caravan. This was once again based on the Bedford CA, but this was not a simple van conversion, the Debonair was an all-GRP-bodied model, which retained only the metal nose cowl of the base vehicle. It was greeted with great delight by the British public and quickly established itself as a Dormobile product of good quality and wonderful design. By the mid-1960s the company was building motor caravans upon just about every marque of light commercial base vehicle; but Dormobile production was not the sole purpose of the Folkestone concern. The company had its own stove-enamelling plant (Land Rover Dormobile cabinets were stove-enamelled) and, when it was not in use for Dormobile products, the bodies of electric fires were produced for another company. The fibreglass department, as well as producing the two-piece mould for the Debonair motor caravan, also manufactured sinks and kitchen cabinets for other models. Martin Walter Ltd also had a contract with the General Post Office during the 1960s to modify Ford Transits and Land Rovers by the addition of items

such as bulkheads and towing brackets. The company was also involved with restoration work to clients' vehicles once produced by them, such as the restoration of Rolls-Royce and Wingham cabriolets (featuring Martin Walter bodywork). In another section of the Folkestone works a number of staff were employed to 'de-wax' all new Alfa Romeo cars arriving in the United Kingdom, and an inspector employed by Alfa Romeo worked in the factory for this purpose. Never a company to stand still, Martin Walter also negotiated the rights during the 1960s for companies in both the USA and Australia to assemble Dormobile motor caravans (from kit form) under licence. This related mostly to Land Rover and Bedford CA models. At the peak of their success Martin Walter Ltd employed around 1,200 at their premises in Cheriton Road and Tile Kiln Lane, in addition to several car showrooms in Kent.

In the 1960s Martin Walter Ltd of Folkestone and Caravans International Motorised (CI/M) of Poole became the British market leaders in motor caravan production. These two giants of the British leisure vehicle industry had much in common: both were based on the English south coast, both had enormous factory facilities employing huge work-

LEFT: *This advertisement dates from 1955 and clearly demonstrates that the owner would always have a bedroom if he or she purchased the 'Dormobile Junior'. This was the name given to the utility version of the Morris Minor van, but similar conversions were available on many light commercials of the time, such as the Standard and the Vauxhall estate car.*

THE NEW BEDFORD DORMOBILE CARAVAN

ABOVE: *The first fully-fitted Dormobile Caravan as seen on the front cover of the 1958 sales brochure. The small rising roof and round porthole rear window were typical features of the early conversions. The first Dormobile Caravans on the Bedford CA also had wooden interior cabinets; note the wooden tray attached to the inside of the rear door.*

LEFT: The Martin Walter factory situated on the Cheriton Road, Folkestone. This was home to all of their utility vehicle conversions up to 1955. As production increased and Dormobile sales were rising, this factory proved to be too small and new premises were purchased in Tile Kiln Lane.

forces and each was producing motor caravans on just about every chassis available. But the bubble was to burst on the booming British economy in the early 1970s with the introduction of value added tax (VAT) in 1973. Much of industry was put on a three-day week, electricity supply cuts dragged on for weeks and fuel rationing became an accepted way of life. The effect on a once buoyant motor caravan industry was devastating, since before this the sale of new motor caravans had been exceeding 15,000 units a year, with that figure widely expected to rise to 17,000 by 1974. As a consequence, production figures tumbled, and many smaller motor caravan producers ceased to trade. Both Dormobile Ltd (by now a separate entity, but still part of the Martin Walter Group) and CI Autohomes (formerly CI/M) did weather the storm, but not without severe losses to their workforces, and the sale of some land and factory areas. Dormobile Ltd in particular had the financial resources of the Charrington Group behind them, of which they had become part in 1973. By coincidence, at this time of hardship a new managing director was brought in to restructure the

RIGHT: The drive outside the factory. This is the front cover of a booklet produced by Martin Walter Ltd, entitled The House of Walter *and released in 1960.*

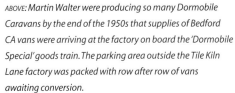

ABOVE: Martin Walter were producing so many Dormobile Caravans by the end of the 1950s that supplies of Bedford CA vans were arriving at the factory on board the 'Dormobile Special' goods train. The parking area outside the Tile Kiln Lane factory was packed with row after row of vans awaiting conversion.

LEFT: A ceremony befitting the occasion; even the local mayor was in attendance. The sign on top of the Bedford really tells the story: 10,000 Bedford conversions in a year of varying forms (not all Dormobile Caravans). On the right of the Bedford is H. Spencer Apps, by this time the grand old man of Martin Walter Ltd. Other board members can be seen on the left.

company and plan for a difficult future; he was John Howell, recruited from CI Autohomes, the main competitor of Dormobile Ltd. John Wade, who had began his career as a Dormobile apprentice, was appointed as the sales manager.

By 1977 Dormobile had managed to come through this difficult time by building not only motor caravans but also public service vehicles, these ranging from twenty-five-seater buses, through to complete ambulance conversions. Although this type of vehicle had now become the main source of income for Dormobile, they were still building several camper van models, but the mould was cast really as far as future conversions were concerned and the only two new motor caravans which followed

were the coachbuilt Deauville and the panel van Toyota Dormobile. That once great workforce, which had numbered 1,200 at the peak of production in the 1960s, was now fewer than 200. The land on which the Dormobile factory had stood since the mid-1950s had also been sold to raise capital, and then leased back. Dormobile Ltd were by this time part of the Coalite Group.

By the time the 1980s had ended the company were no longer producing motor caravans, all of their output was based on converting buses and welfare vehicles. In May 1991 a press release announced that 180 jobs were in the balance as the company had gone into receivership. By 3 June the company had been sold as a going concern, but

sixty-two employees had lost their jobs. A further press report at the end of July announced that a London-based company had purchased Dormobile and added that they hoped to extend the range of vehicles converted at the factory. During the ensuing twelve months further snippets of information about the company appeared in the local Kent press and on regional television reports. All of the news related to factory problems about further job cuts and employees arriving at work only to find the gates locked. This all came to a head on 27 November 1993, when it was reported on regional television that the Dormobile factory had been visited by High Court bailiffs who had seized office equipment; the report also stated that there were growing fears for the future of nearly 200 Dormobile employees. Finally, in 1994 the famous Dormobile factory closed its doors for the final time; it was the end of an illustrious era at the Tile Kiln Lane site. By a strange coincidence, the once great rival of Dormobile in the British leisure market, CI Autohomes of Poole, also ceased to trade in the mid-1990s, and the country had lost not one but two major names from the motor caravan industry in quick succession.

The huge factory site off Tile Kiln Lane has since been redeveloped into a business park and the large expanse of land has been cleared of the old Dormobile buildings. This parcel of land is just a stone's throw from where the Channel Tunnel terminal is situated. The site is now divided into smaller sections on which have been built new business properties, all served by a series of new roads.

ABOVE: This picture dates from 1984 and the familiar interior of the Folkestone factory is by this time home to the conversion of small buses and welfare vehicles. Typical of those was the Ford Transit, often featuring a rear tailgate lift for wheelchair access. A large number of these vehicles have survived and are still in use today, both for their intended purpose, and as home-converted camper vans.

The Tile Kiln Lane factory pictured in the late 1980s. There were still rows of vehicles awaiting conversion, but by this time it was not conversion to camper vans. Coach, minibus and bus were the order of the day, but after several industrial disputes, company changes and takeovers, the writing was on the wall for the famous Folkestone-based firm and complete closure came in the early 1990s.

base vehicle specifications

ABOVE: *Martin Walter Ltd and Dormobile Ltd produced more camper vans on the Bedford CA base than any other converter between 1952 and 1969. The picture on the left shows the early Bedford CA with the split-windscreen and large wheels/tyres. The picture on the right illustrates how the model had changed by 1959, with some modifications to the front-end styling and one-piece, shallow windscreen. By 1964 further modifications to the CA van included an enlarged windscreen, restyled front grille, new dashboard and other refinements; it finally ceased production in 1969.*

RIGHT: *The Bedford CA was phased out and replaced by the CF model seen here. This is the Dormobile Romany II, a panel van conversion with the famous side-hinged, rising roof. Dormobile Ltd built a huge number of their caravan conversions using the CF base, the Freeway and the Land Cruiser being two of the most popular. Although Dormobile stopped using the CF for camper conversions by the late 1970s, they continued to use it for Utilibus models until it was deleted in 1987.*

OVERVIEW

Few if any British motor caravan converters used such a diverse range of base vehicle chassis over the years as Martin Walter Ltd/Dormobile. Today, of course, many people associate the company with the Bedford CA and later CF models, but, from the birth of the British camper van during the mid-1950s, right through to the final Dormobile camper of the early 1980s, the Folkestone factory utilized every popular light commercial chassis for transition from van to leisure vehicle. Those very first Martin Walter vehicles that were given the famous 'Dormobile' name were simply popular estate cars of the period, which had ingenious seats fitted into them in order that the huge luggage space could double up as a large bed. These Dormobile estate cars were bereft of all camping facilities such as cooker, sink and cupboards.

The base vehicles used for motor caravan construction were rather limited in the United Kingdom when this leisure activity first became popular. During the mid-1950s the small number of British-based converters had only a handful of chassis from which to choose, these included the Bedford CA, BMC J2, Ford Thames and the VW Microbus and Kombi. The little Standard Atlas joined this list from 1958. All of these base vehicles really did have something of a monopoly until the introduction of the Rootes Commer 1500 in 1960. The start of the 1960s also saw another new entrant into the base vehicle stakes, the BMC J4. But, despite its popularity as a delivery goods van, it never really found favour with motor caravan converters, and Martin Walter certainly produced one of the most popular conversions upon it. The base vehicle options would remain largely unchanged until the introduction of a motoring legend in 1965, the Ford Transit.

Since its introduction in 1960, the Rootes Commer 1500 (Chrysler Commer from 1964) had become the number one choice as a base vehicle for motor caravan construction, but the new offer-

ing from Ford changed all that. The new Transit could not have been more different from its predecessor, the diminutive Thames. Here at last was a light commercial van that actually had car-like handling, very comfortable seating and later came in a bewildering array of engine and body options – it was indeed a converter's dream chassis.

From this point until 1969 there was once again a period of few technical changes as the Bedford CA, BMC J2 (ceased production in 1967), the Commer and the VW (the panel van model now being the converter's choice over the earlier Microbus and Kombi) dominated sales. The latter part of 1969 saw a new entrant into the option list when a replacement was announced for the ageing Bedford CA. The Bedford CF had arrived and made an immediate impact upon the motor caravan market; in fact Martin Walter Ltd (Dormobile) had remained so loyal to the Bedford brand, that Dormobile models on the new CF were unveiled to the press before the official launch of the entire

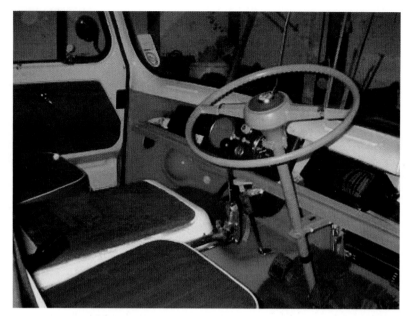

CF range. Converters welcomed the new CF; in a league table of sales for this period it was now the Bedford CF, Commer, Ford Transit and VW out in front.

It is worth emphasizing here the number of BMC base vehicles that were being utilized. For out of all the manufacturers of light vans it was certainly BMC who had the most models available. The Austin 152/Morris J2 (commonly referred to as the J2 range) was not produced after 1967; the model was replaced by the BMC 250JU. As a result of company amalgamations (and a little badge engineering) the Standard Atlas ceased production in 1962, but reappeared immediately as the Leyland 20 (which, in turn, was deleted in 1968). The BMC J4 model introduced in 1960 continued in production until 1974, it then became (with some modifications) the Leyland Sherpa.

The other popular base vehicles used during the 1960s and the 1970s were the Bedford HA, Ford Escort van, Fiat 850/900 van, Land Rover and the MkI Toyota Hiace. Even the little Renault Estafette (not marketed in the United Kingdom) was used for one conversion, the Estafette Touriste, although Martin Walter saw fit not to use this French chassis, assuming (quite correctly) that to obtain spares for it would be a problem here.

It would be fair to say that Martin Walter Ltd did offer the motor caravan buyers the most choice of base vehicles from day one. From the 1950s they were offering conversions upon the Austin-Morris J2, Bedford CA, Ford Thames and Standard Atlas. By the beginning of the

The STANDARD ATLAS 10/12 cwt.

1960s that choice had extended to the BMC J4, Commer, Land Rover and Volkswagen. It seemed that as soon as a new chassis was available for conversion to camper van then the designers at Folkestone were put to work in order to add another Dormobile to their long buyers' list. This continued throughout the 1960s with the Ford Transit, BMC 250JU, Ford Escort and Bedford HA, and, from the end of the decade, the Bedford CF.

BACKGROUND HISTORY OF THE MOST POPULAR BASE VEHICLES

Many of the best selling motor caravans of the Martin Walter Ltd/Dormobile period were based on just six vehicles – the Bedford CA and CF, BMC J2 (Austin and Morris), Commer PA/PB, Ford Transit and, of course, the iconic Volkswagen. In this section I give a more detailed insight into the six leading base vehicles and specification changes during their production.

Specifications of the Popular Base Vehicles/Chassis Used by Martin Walter Ltd

The base vehicles featured in the specifications listing represent the most popular used by the Folkestone company during the classic years of motor caravan production; not included are those used for one-off specials/custom builds and for limited build runs.

Bedford CA 1952–69

Engine: 1508cc, 1595cc petrol engines (4-cylinder diesel option available)

Transmission: 3- and 4-speed column change

Bedford CF 1969–87

Engine (petrol): 1599cc, 1975cc, 1759cc, 2279cc engines

Engine (diesel): 1760cc (Perkins), 2064cc (GM) and 2260cc from 1980

Transmission: 4-speed, floor-mounted change as standard, overdrive option on the CF250 petrol model; 5-speed ZF gearbox was optional on the CF280, CF350 and CF350L models; a GM 3-speed automatic box was optional on all but the CF350 and the CF350L model

Bedford HA 1964–82

Engine: 1256cc petrol engine

Transmission: 4-speed, floor-mounted change

BMC (including later BLMC and Leyland models) Austin 152 (and Morris J2) 1956–67

Engine: 1489cc, 1622cc petrol (diesel option available)

Transmission: 4-speed column change

Austin J4 (also badged as Morris and BMC) 1960–74

Engine: 1622cc petrol (1489cc diesel option available)

Transmission: 4-speed, floor-mounted change

BMC 250JU (renamed Austin-Morris in 1970) 1967–74

Engine: as for the J2 and the J4 model, but engine was relocated at an angle beneath front seats

Transmission: 4-speed

BMC half-ton van (badged as Austin A55 and Morris A60) 1958–71

Engine: 1622cc petrol engine

Transmission: 4-speed column change

Leyland Sherpa 1975–81 (then renamed the Freight Rover Sherpa)

Engine: 1622cc, 1798cc petrol (1798cc diesel option available)

Transmission: 4-speed, floor-mounted change (overdrive became an option on the 1798cc petrol models)

Standard Atlas (later renamed Leyland 20)

Engine: 948cc Standard petrol engine initially, later the 1630cc petrol unit and optional 2260cc diesel engine

Transmission: manual

Land Rover 1948 to the present

Engine: 2286cc petrol engine

Transmission: eight gears (4 × 4)

Commer PA/PB 1500 and 2500 1960–82

Engine: 1494cc, 1592cc, 1725cc petrol engines; Perkins diesel engine was an option

Transmission: 4-speed, floor-mounted change, overdrive being an option on the 1725cc engine.

Fiat 850T and 900T 1956–80

Engine: 903cc petrol unit

Transmission: 4-speed, floor-mounted change

Ford Escort (only the MkI model used for conversion) 1968–75

Engine: 1298cc petrol engine

Transmission: 4-speed, floor-mounted change

Ford Thames 12 and 15cwt range 1957–65

Engine: 1703cc petrol engine; Perkins diesel unit was optional

Transmission: 3- and 4-speed, column-mounted change

Ford Transit 1965 to the present

Engine: petrol options were 1.6-litre, 1.7-litre, 2.0-litre, 2.5-litre and 3.0-litre; diesel options were the Perkins 4/99 and 4/108, also the York 2.4-litre (these were the engine options offered during the 'classic' years, as covered in this book)

Transmission: 4-speed, floor-mounted change, optional overdrive on many engines

Toyota Hi-ace

Engine: 1587cc petrol engine

Transmission: 4-speed, column-mounted change

Volkswagen (Kombi, Microbus and van) 1949–67 (splitscreen models) and 1967–79 (bay window models)

Engine: 1192cc, 1584cc, 1.7-litre, 1.8-litre and 2.0-litre petrol engines

Transmission: 4-speed, floor-mounted change

When Ford ended production of the Thames 400E in 1965 they introduced the Transit range. Martin Walter Ltd were quick off the mark and had soon adapted a version of the Dormobile Caravan. Their initial Transit camper vans simply went under the name of 'Dormobile Transit', but over the next couple of years the Transit Explorer, Enterprise and Freeway camper vans were introduced.

Bedford CA

Vauxhall Motors of Luton introduced this light commercial van in April 1952 in 10/12cwt forms (a 15cwt model was released in 1958) and it quickly established itself as a very popular delivery vehicle. The vehicle enjoyed a seventeen-year production run, before being replaced by the Bedford CF in 1969.

The Bedford CA was a model that was constantly updated throughout production, the most noticeable external modification being the windscreen. When released the CA was fitted with a two-piece 'split screen', this was replaced by a one-piece screen in 1959, together with a redesigned front grille. The windscreen was widened again by June of the same year; it would remain at this size until 1964 when it was increased again in height and width. As far as the power plant was concerned, the CA began with a 1508cc petrol unit (1952–63), which was replaced by a larger 1595cc engine from 1963. Two diesel engines were offered as options during CA production, these were, first, the Perkins 4.99 (from June 1961), and later (1965 onwards) the Perkins 4.108. The wheels fitted to the CA were altered, beginning with 16in on its release, changing to 15in in 1957. By 1960 the sizes were changed once again when the smaller 13in were introduced.

From the outset in 1952 the CA was constantly updated and modified, this included engine size alterations and wheels, body and mechanical changes. The biggest of these changes came in 1964 when the MkII version was announced (although not introduced until May 1965). All CA variants featured 3- and 4-speed, column-mounted gear change. The CA range was discontinued in 1969 when the all-new CF range was introduced.

The CA, despite being a popular vehicle, gained such an excellent reputation within motor caravanning only through the Dormobile conversions. Despite the conversions made by other companies, such as the Hadrian, Calthorpe, Pegasus and Bedmobile, the CA will be forever associated with the great Folkestone company of Martin Walter Ltd (Dormobile).

Bedford CF

As already mentioned, the CF model was a direct replacement for the previously successful CA. At first the CF range used the 1599cc and the 1975cc petrol engines, with the Perkins 1760cc being the diesel option. By 1972 the petrol engine sizes had been increased to 1759 and 2279cc. The engine position in the CF remained similar to that in the old CA model, being mounted half in the cab and half under the front bonnet. The option of sliding cab doors (as seen on the earlier CA) was again available on the CF range, though this feature on the CF in particular was more popular on goods delivery vans than on those converted into motor caravans.

Most motor caravans were built on either the CF220 or the CF250 base (these numbers represented the gross vehicle weight (GVW), for example, the 220 meant 2.20 tons). The designation badge was carried on the front wheel arch. The majority of motor caravans were based on the single rear wheel CF bases; some of the later, much larger, coach-built examples involved the twin rear wheelbase.

The CF range continued to undergo minor alterations and modifications until 1980; in that year the CF was given a facelift. A plastic front grille was the most noticeable external change; the range was also modified and consisted of the CF230, 250, 280 and 350. This revamped model is often incorrectly referred to as the CF2, in fact, the official CF2 was not introduced until 1984. The CF production run ended in 1987, having enjoyed an eighteen-year span, but by this time Dormobile were using it only as a base for welfare-passenger vehicles.

BMC J2 (Austin and Morris Variants)

The J-series formed the basis of the BMC light commercial range, having its origins in the Morris Company. The Austin-Morris merger during the early 1950s saw such models such as the LD, J2 and later 250JU designated as either Austin or Morris.

In 1956 the J2 15cwt model was BMC's first unitary construction van. The company were, and still are, famous for their 'badge engineering', and the J2 was to prove no exception with both Austin and Morris examples being made available. The only real difference between the two was in the lower front panel. Morris versions were given an inverted, heart-shaped grille; Austin variants had a rectangular grille. Originally the range was fitted with the 1489cc B-series petrol engine and received the 1622cc engine in 1961. The range came with a four-speed gearbox as standard and had a column-mounted gear change.

As with the majority of light commercials, the J2 was released in several forms, including the pickup, minibus and van. It was the minibus option that proved popular immediately with motor caravan converters as it came with side windows and a convenient, side-opening door (in addition to the one-piece rear door).

Memorable conversions on the J2 included such models as the Auto-Sleeper, Car-Camper, Cotswold, Highwayman and Paralanian. The J2 was also popular as a base for DIY conversion during the late 1950s and the early 1960s. Martin Walter Ltd converted the BMC J2 during the late 1950s, offering it as an option alongside the Bedford CA camper.

Commer 1500/2500 PA/PB

The Commer 1500 forward-control light van was released in January 1960 and originally powered by the 1494cc petrol engine. This was quickly found to be rather underpowered and was replaced by the 1592cc unit in 1961. The 1500 designation indicated the payload (three-quarters of a ton), and in 1962 it was joined in the model line by the 2500 (1-ton model, payload). By 1964 the Rootes Company had linked with the American Chrysler Corporation; the model was then switched from being the Rootes Commer to the Chrysler Commer.

In 1965 the Commer was given a minor facelift, the successful 1725cc petrol engine was fitted as standard, the front grille was altered and it was given the 'PA' designation. More changes followed in 1967, when the handbrake was relocated from the rear wheels to the front wheels; from this point on the PA became the PB.

Automatic transmission became available from 1965, the Commer having a four-speed, floor-mounted gear change throughout its production (an overdrive became available as an option during the 1970s). The option of a diesel engine was available; at first this was a Perkins 4.99 from 1960, and in 1965 the Perkins 4.108 was offered.

The Commer, having come under Chrysler control, had two other owners before it ceased production in 1982. First the Peugeot Citroen PSA Group became custodians of the Commer brand, but in the final years Renault UK took over the Commer-Dodge mantle; they now hold all production records for the Commer-Dodge vans.

In basic body shape the Commer changed little during its twenty-two-year production run, the most noticeable change taking place in 1976 when the Commer was renamed the Dodge-Spacevan. At this time the front panel was altered, chrome and aluminium trim giving way to plastic. By the time the Commer had become the Dodge Spacevan, Dormobile did not offer any camper van options based on it.

Ford Transit

The Transit name has now become synonymous with light commercial vehicles since its launch in 1965. The Transit was a direct replacement for the Thames, which had been in production for only a few years. The new Transit (named the Thames on its release) really did take the motor caravan industry by storm, not to mention the warm reception it received from those in the trade. At the time of its introduction no fewer than forty-four different versions, built on six models, were available, ranging in payload capacity from 12 to 35cwt. The list of the bases available was equally as impressive, including van, custom van, kombi, bus, custom bus, chassis cab, custom chassis cab and chassis windshield. So varied were the Transit options that Ford claimed to offer a thousand bodywork options, and added that they could build over six million Transits without ever building two exactly the same.

The engines fitted to the Transit have been as varied as the bodywork options over the years, ranging from 1.7- to 3.0-litre petrol, together with a variety of diesel options. To say that the Transit went through several modifications over the years would be a huge understatement, I shall therefore simply highlight some of the more major changes. The transmission on the Transit was a four-speed, floor-mounted gear change on all models; from 1967 a Borg Warner automatic gearbox became optionally available. In 1968 the interior cab layout was modified after Ford had conducted some extensive safety checks. The facia was redesigned, the heater controls repositioned and additional padding and rocker-type switches fitted. By June 1968 Ford were offering the high compression V4 2-litre-engine (petrol), which became the most common unit fitted in motor caravan conversions. A bigger petrol engine became an option in 1974 with the 3.0-litre V6; front disc brakes were also added to the options listed that year. The original MkI Transit would be a story of constant modification until 1978 when Ford announced the MkII model. The new Transit featured a completely new cab interior and restyling to the front cab panels, including the ubiquitous 1970s plastic grille.

Volkswagen

Of all the base vehicles used for conversion to camper van throughout the classic years it is the VW that has remained the most popular, and in consequence it now enjoys iconic status. The first camper conversions to appear on the VW were carried out by the German Westfalia company in 1951 and its early 'camping boxes' (with limited interior fixtures) became an instant hit. By 1955 Westfalia had introduced fully-fitted models with sink, cooker, bed and storage cupboards, and in the United Kingdom it was Peter Pitt who converted the first VW, with Jack White of Devon Conversions following a year later in 1957. Other conversions quickly followed, including the Moortown and European Cars.

Many enthusiasts of classic VW camper vans regard the marriage between the splitscreen VW and Martin Walter Ltd as the ultimate British conversion, and the first VW Dormobile appeared in 1961 based on the Microbus (bulkhead model). With facilities such as the cooker placed at the rear of the vehicle and the cavernous Dormobile rising roof, this model gave the impression of having a spacious interior. But by the time that the bay window VW van was introduced in 1968, Dormobile had completely altered the internal layout. The company used the VW Kombi van for this and gave it the model number D4/6. By 1970 Dormobile had added the D4/8 model to its range. This was primarily a people carrier and was based on either the Kombi or the Microbus van. As the Dormobile model number suggests, it was designed to sleep four and to carry eight, hence the code D4/8, but, being aimed at the economy market, the interior caravan fittings were rather basic.

Without question the most popular Dormobile camper van of the present day, in both the early (split screen) and the later (D4/6) form.

3 *Bedford Romany* (Dormobile Caravan)

ABOVE: Ralph Woodbridge owns this 1967 Dormobile Romany De Luxe. This particular example is completely unrestored and still carries its original paintwork. The exterior is something of a dilemma for Ralph, who likes the originality but realizes that the time is approaching when it may have to have some welding repairs and a new coat of paint.

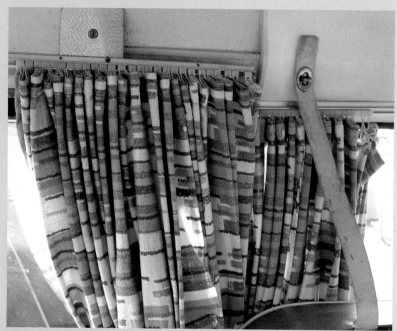

There cannot be too many Dormobile examples from the 1960s that still sport their original Martin Walter curtains. In varying colour schemes, this pattern was used often at this time. The strap with the turn-buckle fastening is holding the rear seat up against the side of the vehicle in order to provide extra floor space.

ROMANY-BEDFORD CA

It was quite possibly the model from the classic years of British motor-caravanning that became such an iconic image. That candy-stripe canvas roof, hinged high in the air from one side of the vehicle really conjures up an image of a bygone era, and I am, of course, referring to the famous patented Dormobile rising roof as fitted to many Dormobile models from the mid-1950s. In the raised position one knew instantly, even from a great distance, that it must be a Dormobile motor caravan (although it was used under licence by a couple of other converters). It was not the first rising roof to be fitted to a conversion (that honour went to Calthorpe), but it certainly became the enduring image of 1950s and 1960s camp sites around Britain.

The first Martin Walter motor caravan to be so fitted was the 'Dormobile Caravan' in 1957, a conversion of the popular Bedford CA light van. This was the model that would put the names of both Martin Walter Ltd and Dormobile well on the map. The company

That rear seat is seen here, folded against the interior side. The red upholstery with white piping is original. The ingenious Dormatic seat mechanism can be clearly seen in this picture.

BELOW: The seat on the opposite side of the vehicle, once again folded up. Note the passenger seat in the rearward-facing position, but without the table in position.

BELOW LEFT: The table in place in the space immediately behind the passenger seat. In this picture the passenger seat and the rear seat are arranged for dining, with the two adjacent seats laid flat in bench style. The original table leg is the metal tube at the end; the metal bracket hanging down is a modification made by the owner in order to mount the table sideways, and is a secondary leg.

BELOW RIGHT: The Formica-topped Dormobile table fastened against the side of the vehicle with a retaining clip. The sliding side window also on view here was standard on Dormobile Romany models.

LEFT: The driving cab of the Bedford CA Dormobile Romany was quite sparse with most of the metal finish still on show. Seen here, the driver's seat is folded flat; this, with the addition of the rear seat in a similar position, would form one of the single beds. Cab windows had sliding glass, as opposed to window winders.

BELOW LEFT: This picture demonstrates that the Bedford CA Romany was at the economy end of the sales market, at least in basic or De Luxe finish. The kitchen facilities were limited, with a simple, two-burner hob and grill, and a plastic sink alongside. The finish to the Melamine cabinets is a light grey wood-grain effect.

BOTTOM LEFT: Storage in the Romany had to be well planned. On the kitchen side of the interior there were only a couple of spaces beneath the cooker and the sink, and this glass-fronted unit above the cooker.

already had a utility vehicle in production based on the Bedford CA, featuring their famous Dormatic seats, which could be altered into several positions, and, in addition, be laid flat to form a bed. Once some simple interior fittings and the rising roof were added it became a motor caravan. But even the Martin Walter company must have been a little surprised at the instant success of their creation. It quickly gained rave reviews in the motoring press, not least because it was pitched at an affordable price; the fact that it happened to be based upon the most popular light van of the time, the CA, also helped considerably. In this period of post-war Britain the people were again beginning to take part in leisure activities on a greater scale – trailer caravans had enjoyed a huge success previously and now it was the turn of the motorized caravan to gain in popularity. The launch of the Dormobile Caravan on the Bedford CA fitted in perfectly with the growth of the British economy, the two went hand in hand, and a legend was born.

To this day those early models remain pleasing to look at, with their round porthole window in the side and the early version of that famous rising roof. Throughout the late 1950s the company kept the price of this model to a minimum in order to maximize sales, and it was one of the lowest priced models on the annual listings/buyers guides. In 1958 (in standard form) the cost of a Dormobile Caravan was £725, beating its two nearest rivals, the Calthorpe Home-Cruiser and the Pitt Moto-Caravan. The giant Martin Walter concern did, of course, have a head start on their rivals during the 1950s – they were already well established coachbuilders, had huge factory premises and a trained workforce. Add to these factors their long-standing relationship with Vauxhall Motors, and you have a recipe for undoubted success – as long as you have the goods to market in the first instance, and they certainly did. In terms of sales, the Dormobile Caravan left all the other British models trailing; it really was in a league of its own. In fact, such was the demand for Martin Walter Bedford CA conversions (both the Utility van and the Dormobile Caravan) that base vehicles were transported by a direct rail link from Luton (Vauxhall) to the Martin Walter factory in Folkestone. One figure certainly worth stating here concerns Bedford CA conversion by the company in 1959: in that year alone they carried out 10,000 conversions, which included the Dormobile Caravan, the Utilabrake, the Utilicon, the Utilabus and the Workobus.

By the start of the 1960s the famous Dormobile rising roof had been enlarged, and the Dormobile Caravan was now known as the Romany. By the time the company put on its display at that year's Motor Show their model line-up numbered fifteen examples on six different base vehicles. But, despite extending their range of models, it remained the Romany that was the most favoured by the buyers. The Romany range actually comprised five options. First the Romany 'Standard', a Bedford CAS (short-wheel-base model) with a fixed factory metal roof; next the Romany 'Super', again on the Bedford CAS model but now fitted with a rising roof. These two models were then duplicated, but this time on the Bedford CAL (long-wheel-base model). The top of the Romany range was the 'De Luxe', based on the Bedford CAL; this model had both a rising roof and a roof rack built on to the frontal roof area, giving a sleek and streamlined appearance. Adding to the attractive external appearance of the De Luxe model were GRP tail fins fitted on the rear sides of the vehicle. This Romany range, in 1964, varied in price from £658 for the Standard through to £888 for the

The view of the roof and the roof bunk from the rear step. The bunks were slightly tapered at one end in order to aid access to them at night. During the day these bunks would be rolled up and clipped to the side of the roof aperture.

This little step/stool is a typical Dormobile trademark. It pulled out from the base of the wardrobe and was held in place by a metal leg. This was used to aid access up to the bunks in the roof space and also as a stool for the cook when sitting opposite the cooker. Note the tiny 'Easicool' cabinet in the corner; this did and indeed still does work quite well – it was an optional extra and not fitted as standard equipment. The two plastic water containers would originally have been placed on top of the cooler cabinet and held in place with the strap pictured.

ABOVE: *This 1967 Romany might well be original but it is now showing signs of its age, evident here with its many stone chips and scratches. The metal badge proudly proclaims what this camper is.*

RIGHT: *The early Bedford Dormobile Caravan was quite different from the later Romany models. This Martin Walter publicity picture dates from the end of 1958 and clearly demonstrates the larger rising roof, which provided the option of roof bunks. This early roof also differs from later versions in that it had two rectangular opening windows, and the contour of the GRP moulding had yet to take on the design of the more familiar shape. Note also the small, round, porthole window with bevelled glass, a regular feature of early Dormobile camper vans and also seen on the Ford Thames and BMC J2 of this period.*

De Luxe. As if this Romany range was not confusing enough, another Bedford CA model was offered at £995. This was the 'Deauville'; it had most of the features found in and on the De Luxe offering but the interior was finished in real wood, as opposed to the laminate-faced cupboards of the other models.

Throughout the 1960s the Dormobile Romany continued to be the biggest selling panel van conversion in the United Kingdom. The model name was eventually carried over to the Bedford CF when it replaced the CA in 1969.

For the purposes of description I shall concentrate on the Bedford CA Romany from 1967, since by this time it had undergone considerable changes from the early example. The Romany was a four-door model featuring sliding cab doors and twin opening rear doors. With the exception of the Dormatic seats and their variable positioning, the interior was of the traditional panel van layout. Looking toward the cab from the rear, there was a kitchen on the left fitted with a sink, two-burner hob with grill, with a drawer and storage cupboards below. A water carrier was situated on the end, nearest the rear doors, which supplied water to the sink via a hand pump. On the opposite side from the kitchen was a wardrobe and further storage unit. The base of the wardrobe incorporated a pull-out stool/seat for use when one was cooking. All the units in the Romany Standard and Super models were of a light wood-effect laminate. Fitted along both vehicle sides were long windows with sliding panels, and a Dormobile 'air-scoop' window was placed near the cooker to aid in the expulsion of cooking smells and the prevention of condensation.

The forward dinette/seating area was centred on the famous Dormatic seats, which were capable of being turned every which way imaginable. Not only could they face forward and reverse, it was also possible to fold them up completely against the vehicle sides in order to carry bulky items. At night these seats could be altered to form either two single beds or one double. Two stretcher bunks were housed in the cavernous rising roof. The floor covering in the Romany range differed between each model: linoleum, rubber and PVC coverings were used. The two gas cylinders were held in special compartments in the vehicle floor, a metal container was also housed in the floor and this could be used either for further storage or a chemical toilet.

The large, side-hinged Dormobile rising roof gave ample standing room in

Alan Kirtley of Bedfordshire is a keen enthusiast of all Dormobile models, having owned several over the years. He has recently restored this 1958 model. It is seen here on display at the British Classic Motor Show looking resplendent in its new livery. This is the MkI version of the famous Dormobile roof, quite small at this stage, with just a single opening vent on top.

The same vehicle, this time viewed from the front. Being the early
CA Bedford, this one is fitted with the split windscreen arrangement.
The small rising roof is evident here.

An alternative view of the early Dormobile roof, as seen from the rear. The
idea (according to a past Dormobile designer) came from the hoods seen
on old children's prams of the time, and thus in the trade became known as
the 'pram style' hood. A Dormobile designer from the time advised me that
the idea for the candy-stripe material came about more by accident than
planning, and was simply a material held in store at the time.

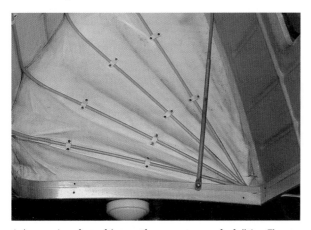

A close-up view of one of the most famous camper roofs of all time. The
'pram' hoops are clearly visible here, held in place with plastic retaining clips
and riveted through the roof material. If this roof had one drawback it was
the amount of condensation that would drip on the occupants from above.
On much later versions of the roof the designers incorporated an inner
(breathable) lining in order to overcome this problem.

The opening 'side-scoop' window, which would swivel on a central pin top
and bottom. This window was a Dormobile feature throughout the 1950s,
1960s and 1970s.

Some might say that the interior of the early Bedford Dormobile was rather
spartan, perhaps even crude. But it is well to remember that this was in the
1950s and Martin Walter were aiming this model at the cheaper end of the
motorcaravan market. On a personal note, I prefer this early wooden
interior to the later mass-produced Melamine finish. But no doubt this one
was more labour-intensive and thus not economical to produce.

The rear corner of the same model showing the petrol filler flap and the
wheel 'spat' half obscuring the rear wheel. A nice Dormobile coach line
breaks up the side appearance and continues around under the rear doors.

the vehicle and this was fitted with roof lights/ventilators. Curtains were fitted as standard to all windows and electric lighting was another standard fitment. The optional extras available for the Romany were quite extensive, as one would expect from Dormobile. As with most panel van conversions of the period, the list did include a refrigerator. Prices for the Romany in 1967 had risen to £872 for the Super model and £947 for the De Luxe. Due to the large numbers produced over a lengthy period, a large number have survived. But I should point out that many of these Dormobile models have undergone restoration, and some owners have taken that opportunity to make minor changes to them, sometimes adding bits from another model within the range so that few surviving examples will now be in their original, 'factory' condition.

Well-restored driving cab, even if the radio is a modern product. There are few gadgets to distract the 1950s' Dormobile motorist here: two gauges, column gear change, steering wheel and handbrake.

The Union Jack emblem is a later addition at the rear, but the neat folding step is original. The wooden step would fold up against the back of the vehicle and then the whole step mechanism folded into the rear of the camper.

Installed in the Folkestone factory in 1958 and still usable today (after testing by a CORGI-registered engineer), this is the standard, two-burner hob with grill.

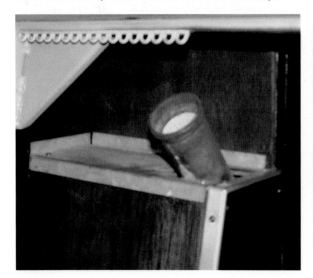

Fresh water on the 1958 model came from a galvanized tank housed in the rear corner. Water was poured in through the filler neck seen here (cap removed as the vehicle was on display).

The water came out of this spout at the base, activated by a valve/tap, a simple gravity feed principle of operation.

ABOVE: No solar-powered lighting for 1950s motorcaravanners! Cooking, reading, washing and dressing were done by gas light, a nice original feature.

RIGHT: The Dormatic seat frames are original in this 1958 example, but the seats have been reupholstered recently with a period-looking material in blue and cream with a matching piping for good effect.

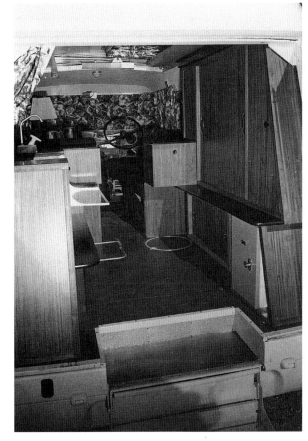

In 1963 Martin Walter Ltd introduced an up-market version of the famous Bedford Dormobile Caravan, the 'Deauville'. With its beautifully finished wooden interior, this model was considerably more expensive than the standard example. It is easy to see why when looking at these pictures, as the interior layout was slightly different from that of other Bedford Caravans.

The two-burner hob/grill and sink were all that remained from the standard model. The cabinet makers at Folkestone produced a fabulous interior on the Deauville model. As one might expect, not that many were produced and they remain highly sought after on the classic scene today.

TOP: *Time for bed in this press picture of the Martin Walter Romany De Luxe four-berth. Even with the beds in position there was still ample space at the rear to reach the kitchen facilities.*

ABOVE: *Time for tea. This press picture for the same model demonstrates the table erected against the side and the seating arranged around it, though access to the table from the rear (and vice versa) was questionable.*

The early (1958) model appearing in many of the illustrations on the previous pages has been restored by Alan Kirtley, of Bedfordshire. He has owned several Dormobile models over the years, including a Bedford HA Roma, a Bedford Debonair, a Bedford Land Cruiser and a Ford Thames.

4

BMC J2 *(Austin A152/Morris J2)*

ABOVE: After Martin Walter released the fully-fitted Bedford Dormobile, the BMC version closely followed. The Austin A152/Morris J2 was a forward-control van with a single hinged rear door and huge load capacity, perfect for conversion into a Dormobile Caravan. An early example (late 1958) is demonstrated here in the Kent countryside on what appears to be a ladies' day out.

BELOW: Side view of the BMC J2 Dormobile Caravan. In addition to the large rear door, this model also had side access with a drop-down entrance step. The Dormobile roof aperture had been cut toward the rear of the vehicle, allowing for the fitting of a roof rack at the front. Customers could order either the Austin or the Morris version depending upon their motoring allegiance.

I have to admit at the outset of this chapter that I have no knowledge of any surviving examples in the United Kingdom of the BMC J2 Dormobile. I made many attempts while preparing this book to trace any examples, either currently in use or under restoration, but my search has been unsuccessful. But I can assure you that the BMC J2 Dormobile did exist, as advertising material and sales brochures from the period will testify.

Martin Walter Ltd released the BMC J2 Dormobile during the late 1950s, and it was available on both BMC variants, the Austin A152 or the Morris J2 (the same vehicle but with differing front panel and marque badge). It is interesting to note that the company actually listed the Austin and the Morris Dormobile separately in publicity material, which was a little odd given that it was basically the same vehicle. I would assume that brand loyalty was

far more important to vehicle buyers in the 1950s, and families who had purchased an Austin car for many years would want to progress to an Austin Dormobile in preference to any other marque.

For the purposes of describing the BMC Dormobile I shall focus my attention on the Austin A152 dating from 1960. This how the Martin Walter company set about advertising the model:

The World Is Your Oyster

The DORMOBILE Caravan permits you to go where you like and when you like, free of towing difficulties, and the expense of hotels – you can drive it to any accessible place you choose – down narrow lanes, up mountain roads. It handles and manoeuvres like a car, and it can be parked in very rough and restricted places owing to its excellent ground clearance and steering lock. It is

LEFT: The interior of the BMC Dormobile Caravan followed the layout used on the Bedford model – kitchen to one side and the wardrobe opposite. In this picture the seats are obviously prepared for sleeping and are in the fold flat position. The BMC Dormobile featured a huge, single rear door.

RIGHT: Tea time once again, this time inside the BMC. The seats maintain their night-time position, but now act as two separate bench seats for the central dining table.

RIGHT: The swinging sixties had arrived, and with them the desire to explore the Continent in a camper van, or so the Martin Walter publicity department were hoping. This advertisement shows the Austin version of the Dormobile Caravan at a price of £877.17s.6d.

ABOVE: Apologies for the poor quality of this picture, but I had to prove that a BMC Dormobile Caravan did once exist. This Morris version was once owned by Bob Darling, a leading light in the Motorcaravanners Club during the early 1960s. The unmistakable Dormobile roof is raised here as the family take a break beside a lake.

ideal for weekend picnic parties for the family, and for attending race meetings and sporting events where it represents a mobile grandstand with refreshment facilities laid on. It is also eminently suitable for travelling representatives and salesmen as a bedroom-cum-office.

Whereas the majority of camper vans built by Martin Walter Ltd were given some wonderful names, this particular model was listed simply as the 'Martin Walter conversion of the Austin A152 van'. This did tend to happen with the early Dormobile Caravan models; the Ford Thames and the Commer were similarly listed. The Austin A152 Dormobile was based on the minibus chassis, featuring windows all around, plus a side-opening door in addition to the one-piece rear door. The Austin was fitted with the patented Dormobile rising roof, and on this model the roof was positioned over the rear end (where the majority of facilities were located). A warning light was fitted to the dashboard of the vehicle to indicate to the driver that the roof was still erect when the ignition was switched on. This model, as with other Dormobile examples, was well ventilated, a large perspex opening vent was fitted to the rising roof and the familiar 'air-scoop' Dormobile windows were fitted to one glass panel on either side of the camper.

A one-piece rear door (with a glazed top half) gave access to the interior, with a built-in rear step to assist. The designers made use of the huge, rear BMC door by adding a rectangular wooden cupboard with a central shelf. At the rear right-hand corner of the Austin was the kitchen unit; this was constructed from a 'glossy plastic wood veneer'. The unit housed a two-burner gas hob with grill, a very small plastic sink alongside and twin opening doors below for storage. Hinged worktops (hinged at the rear) completed this unit, with a Dormobile litter bag in red and white stripes fitted at the side of the unit, nearest to the rear door. Incidentally, these litter bags are now a highly sought after item among Dormobile camper van owners. The cylinders that supplied gas to the cooker/grill were in the traditional Dormobile location, a cradle under the vehicle, accessed via a round hatch in the vehicle floor (one gas cylinder was supplied as part of the standard equipment).

Within the cab of the Austin were two separate, adjustable seats for the driver and passenger, these being the standard seats as fitted by Austin. In the rear of the vehicle were four individual seats of the patented Dormobile design (Dormatic). These four were arranged one behind another, in the forward-facing position with a gangway in between. The rears of these seats could be slid together to form a bench seat. For night-time use, the rear seats could be folded flat within a couple of minutes to form two single beds, and this still left ample room in the vehicle for undressing and dressing, and for providing access to the rear cupboards. The four-berth option of the Austin Dormobile provided two stretcher-type bunk beds

within the large roof space; an additional child's bunk was available for fitting in the cab area, allowing a child to sleep across the width of the vehicle.

Storage space inside the Austin was rather limited, as was the case with many of the early Dormobile caravans. The main storage areas consisted of a wardrobe at the nearside rear, cupboards beneath the cooker and sink, a blanket cupboard on the nearside and a locker built into the rear door. A pair of plastic water containers were supplied as part of the standard equipment, a 4 and a 2gal tank.

At meal times a table was supplied, which was fitted with fold-down legs. For dining, this was positioned in the gangway between the rear seats, which were each folded flat in the single-bed position against the sides of the vehicle. When the table was not in use it was stored flat against the rear of the front bulkhead dividing the cab from the rear quarters. With regard to ancillary items in the Austin Dormobile, curtains were supplied for all windows, an electric light was fitted in the cab area, with an additional light providing illumination to the upper bunk beds, a gas light was situated at the rear offside of the interior and the floor area of the vehicle was fitted with lino material, with carpet for the main gangway as an optional extra.

Continuing the theme of optional extras, a Dormobile tent for fitting to the rear was available, which could sleep a further two people. Other options included a roof rack to cover the cab area, a heater and a radio. When ordering the Austin Dormobile, customers could specify either a red and white roof canvas or a green and white one. Body colour options were many and varied, with a customer being allowed to choose from both the Austin van range and the Martin Walter range.

For an example of prices for this model I quote from the Martin Walter price list issued for the Motor Show of 1960. At this time the company was offering fifteen Dormobile motor caravans. The price of an Austin two-berth example was £864, with the four-berth model at £879. Having studied this particular price list, it is interesting to note that a couple of larger 'coach-built' models were cheaper than the Austin/Morris Dormobile. The Bluebird Highwayman had a price tag of £875 and the Ford Thames Hadrian was £847. In fact, the Austin four-berth Hadrian model was priced at £866, only £2 more than the Austin/Morris Dormobile two-berth. But it would be safe to assume that any Austin or Morris Dormobile example today would be worth considerably more than its original cost.

ABOVE: Looks can be deceiving. Although this 1958 Morris J2 clearly has a Dormobile roof, it is not a genuine Martin Walter Caravan. This is 'Bertie', which was actually a home-converted camper van. Although never intended to, it did fool some who believed it to be a product of the Folkestone factory.
ABOVE RIGHT: 'Bertie' once more, this time the interior is clearly visible. Its owner Matt Traxton did an excellent job of fitting the Dormobile roof and managing to make the interior look quite 'period'. There is a reason for showing a non-genuine BMC Dormobile Caravan here: I could not trace a real survivor despite months of searching. So if you happen to know of one or, indeed, own one, look after it, it does have real rarity value.

5

Standard Atlas

The original publicity picture for the Martin Walter Dormobile Atlas Major – certainly one of the prettiest light commercial vans ever produced in Britain.

In the rarity stakes the Dormobile conversion based on the Standard Atlas Major 10/12cwt van rates highly. Of all the light commercials produced during the 1950s and the 1960s the Atlas must surely be one of the rarest, certainly as far as survivors are concerned. Few van, pickup and camper van derivatives have withstood the test of time, and although I am aware of a Calthorpe camper and a Kenex conversion, I have been unable to trace a surviving Martin Walter

Dormobile model. Martin Walter Ltd had a penchant for utilizing the majority of the base vehicles available to them, though not all were successful. A case in point was the conversion of the Atlas Major – this was as good as any which they had carried out on other base vehicles, and there was certainly nothing wrong with the result, it was simply that the British public did not take to the Standard Atlas with any degree of warmth. Even in its basic

delivery van form, the Atlas could never be described as a roaring sales success.

The Atlas was launched in 1958 and was originally powered by the diminutive 948cc engine, as fitted to the Standard 10 motor car. The Dormobile conversion based on the Atlas van was similar indeed to that seen on the BMC J2 described in the previous chapter. In fact, the internal layout was largely identical, with the Atlas also available in two- and four-berth models.

ABOVE: Dormobile Caravan on the Atlas once again, this time showing the roof raised and the side entrance door.

ABOVE RIGHT: Apologies for the poor quality of this shot, but with the lack of a 'real' specimen one has to make do. This view depicts the side door entrance and the Dormatic seats folded flat – his would be the position for dining at the table (just visible) and to make the beds up.

The Atlas was, and still is, pleasing on the eye. Externally the roof over the rear load area was slightly higher than that over the cab, creating a rather appealing line. The addition of the famous Dormobile roof complemented the Atlas roof-line quite nicely, while the lower cab roof was the perfect shape for the fitting of a metal roof rack. The sides of the vehicle were given the Dormobile styling treatment, with the addition of eye-catching side flashes in a colour contrasting to that of the main body. The Atlas had a one-piece rear door and a side entry door. Seating inside the Atlas Dormobile consisted of four forward-facing seats of the Dormatic design; these were upholstered in red or blue 'Duracour'. These seats formed two single beds when laid flat, with an extra two stretcher-type bunk beds in the roof space on the four-berth model. In a similar style to the BMC J2 models, the four single seats were laid flat in 'bench' style for dining, with the table situated in the centre gangway.

The kitchen facilities consisted of a two-burner hob with grill and a plastic sink with draining board. The two gas cylinders used to power the hob/grill were positioned in a recessed cradle under the floor. Water for washing and cooking purposes was stored in the two containers supplied as standard, one of 4gal capacity and the other of 2gal. Cupboard and storage facilities were almost identical to those found in the BMC J2 examples, with a cupboard below the hob/grill, wardrobe on the offside rear and a large shelf situated above the cooker. All the cabinet work was finished in a hard-wearing, washable, Melamine plastic veneer. Interior lighting was provided from the electric light in the driving cab area and a 12V fluorescent light in the main living area.

A host of optional extras was available for the Atlas Dormobile, including an Elsan toilet and a gas-operated refrigerator. The Standard Atlas Dormobile was available in a choice of twenty-five different body colours. The wording used to sell motor caravans in sales brochures appears to have altered little over the years; this is how Martin Walter described the Atlas Dormobile on the cover of their sales literature in 1961:

This spacious vehicle with its powerful 1670cc engine is equipped with 2 or 4 berths, a cooker unit complete with sink and cupboards with sliding doors, a wardrobe, water and gas supplies, fluorescent lighting and all other refinements which have helped to earn the Dormobile caravan its fine reputation. The owner of an Atlas Major Dormobile Caravan will have a self-contained unit, capable of Continental touring and a weekend holiday home with car comfort and convenience for everyday driving and parking.

As an illustration of pricing, during the winter of 1960/61 the Atlas Dormobile cost £912 for the two-berth model and £927 for the four-berth example. The Standard Atlas was produced between 1958 and 1962. It was then renamed the Leyland 15-20 and remained in

LEFT: Martin Walter used the 10–12cwt Atlas Major for conversion to Dormobile Caravan. This one also had the slightly more powerful 1670cc engine.

BOTTOM LEFT: Advertising the Atlas Dormobile; not only was I unable to trace any examples of the vehicle, but even finding the literature proved quite difficult (Brian Birch at the Standard Club kindly came to my rescue).

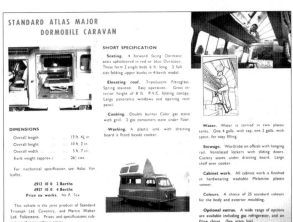

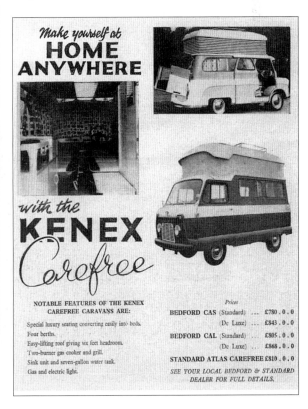

RIGHT: Any Standard Atlas camper van is a rare sight today, and back in the 1950s and 1960s there were few converters using them; one exception was Kenex Coachworks of Dover with their 'Carefree' range of camper vans.

ABOVE: This is a Kenex Carefree camper dating from around 1961 and based on the Standard Atlas. It still remains one of my favourite motoring publicity pictures – a camper van with no registration plate, in a field with cows. The mind boggles as to what the advertising executive was thinking at Kenex.

LEFT: Brian Birch, an archivist for the Standard Motor Club, owns this beautiful Standard Atlas 'Kenebrake' by Kenex. The Atlas in any form must be one of the rarest light commercials of the late 1950s and early 1960s, there are so few survivors. The reason this particular van appears here is because Martin Walter Ltd acquired Kenex Coachworks of Dover around 1963.

production until 1968. The vehicle tooling was all transferred to Standard Motor Products of India in 1968 and the vehicle remained in production throughout the 1970s (though not in camper van form).

Martin Walter Ltd did carry out a camper conversion on the Leyland 20 chassis during the mid-1960s in the form of the Land Cruiser; this is described in greater detail in Chapter 13.

Volkswagen (early model)

ABOVE: My good friend Alan Powell rescued this 1966 splitty Dormobile in 1991 after seeing it advertised in an owners' club journal. It had been purchased by the then owner in Scotland as a donor vehicle for his own VW splitty camper, but he decided that it might just be restorable, and this is when Alan stepped in.

BELOW: Alan had the splitty transported to his Devon home and began to assess its condition. There was little to inspect around the bottom half of the vehicle since it was no longer there. Thankfully all the repairable sections were readily available, and Alan set to with the grinder and welder.

Of all the camper conversions released by Martin Walter Ltd/Dormobile over the years, their conversion of the early Volkswagen 'Splitty' is surely the most in demand on the classic scene today. The iconic Dormobile conversion is highly sought after by enthusiasts of the splitscreen bus worldwide. The first Volkswagen Dormobile was released in 1961 and unveiled to the public at the Motor Show; it had the benefit of having full Volkswagen approval and came with a full VW warranty.

The VW Dormobile was based on the Microbus model with a bulkhead and had the twin opening side doors. The most characteristic feature of this model, as with any Dormobile panel van conversion, was the famous side-hinged, rising roof. On this early VW Dormobile the rising roof was placed over the central area of the original metal factory roof. On this conversion an electrical contact was fitted in order to warn the driver when he was pulling away that the roof might still be in the raised position. The enormous roof also meant that the VW Dormobile was a true four-berth model. As with previous camper conversions from the

The result of all the hard work is clearly evident in this picture, and in 1997 Alan finally had the VW Dormobile back on the road (it had last been used in 1983). The saving grace was that the vehicle had its full original Dormobile interior and rising roof, which happened to be in very good order.

Folkestone factory, the interior was fitted with their Dormatic seating. These seats would fold and slide in every direction, allowing the occupants to have both forward- and rearward-facing seats, with the added benefit that they could also be folded flat to make two single beds or one double. To make this a forerunner to the MPV of today, the Dormatic seats could also be folded up and strapped to the sides of the vehicle, thus allowing any amount of goods to be carried inside on the large floor space.

The kitchen facilities in this early VW Dormobile were situated at the rear of the interior, over the engine bay area. This consisted of a two-burner hob with grill, sink and draining board. Storage cupboards were situated below the hob and sink with a tall wardrobe unit filling the space next to the sink. On early models the hob/grill was situated to the left-rear of the camper, but at the end of 1964 the cooker was moved to the right-hand side. A small folding step was also incorporated into the base of the kitchen unit in order to aid access to the upper bunk beds within the raising roof space. The early kitchen units were made of steel, but this was altered at the end of 1962 when plastic veneer over wood was introduced. The gas for the hob was

The interior layout was far removed from the Dormobile D4/6 design, which was to follow on from the bay window model. In the splitty version all the facilities were located at the rear. The two single rear seats are seen here folded up against the sides of the interior.

Rear units once more with the gas hob on the right-hand side and the sink next to it. On the far left of the picture is the small wardrobe, with additional storage below the hob/sink and above. The rear seats here are laid flat in the double-bed position.

This is the view looking into the camper from the side doors. All seats in the rear have been folded up to allow free floor space for carrying bulky items. A real dual-purpose vehicle, in the Martin Walter tradition.

The same interior set-up, but this time viewed from another angle. The front passenger seats have been tilted forward to create a greater load-carrying space.

housed in a purpose-built carrier in the engine compartment and water was kept in two containers. Water was delivered to the sink via a manual pump-action tap. Interior lighting was supplied from one electric unit at the front of the roof void and another over the rear kitchen. Complementing the interior fitments were a lino floor covering and fitted curtains to all windows. A dining table, with fold-away leg, was supplied as standard; this was fitted in the middle of the camper into a slot on the inner wall of the vehicle.

Although many VW camper enthusiasts automatically think of the early Dormobile models with that distinctive rising roof, a two-berth option did become available from around 1963, though this, of course, restricted interior headroom to the factory-fitted, metal roof. As with the majority of Dormobile camper vans, there was a huge list of optional extras from which to choose; these included chromium-plated bumpers and VW badge, roof rack, screen washers (electric or manual), electric dash clock, fog lamps and a radio. In addition, there was also the optional camping equipment list, which was comprehensive and included everything from an air bed, to awning, and a kettle, through to a full saucepan

ABOVE: All four single rear seats are seen here in the forward-facing position for travelling. Alan is quite rightly proud of the fact that these are all the original seats, still with their original upholstery. There can be few VW Dormobile models still in use from this period with such a claim.

ABOVE RIGHT: The two single rear seats in the travelling position. That glorious Dormobile seat covering is on full view here, I am so pleased that Alan took my advice and did not have the seats recovered.

RIGHT: Rear seats again, but this time arranged for dining (the table was placed in between) or for simply relaxing.

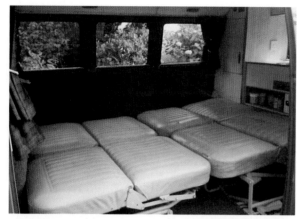

Martin Walter gave these famous seats the name Dormatic; I strongly believe it should have been 'Dormagic'. They are pictured here in the double-bed arrangement. Of course, the rear kitchen facilities were still accessible, even from bed.

ABOVE: *This picture shows the four seats in the sleeping position once more, but this time they are arranged as two single beds.*

LEFT: *One of the most popular rising roofs ever placed on the top of a camper van, this is the view of the Dormobile roof in the raised position with the two bunk beds in place.*

RIGHT: *All genuine Martin Walter Dormobile campers left the factory with a makers' plate on the dashboard and a serial number stamped on the bottom.*

BELOW: *View with the rear tailgate raised. The shelf above the engine bay was useful for the storage of bedding and camping equipment. On the left-hand side is the period cooler cabinet, a Dormobile optional extra. Alan's VW has been fitted with an electric hook-up system, just visible on the right above the orange cable.*

set. In fact, during the 1960s Martin Walter Ltd offered the most complementary list of optional extras of all the British converters.

At the time of its launch, late in 1961, the VW Dormobile had a price tag of £915 in standard form. Colour options on the early models included Dover Blue, Light Grey, Pearl White and Velvet Green; the last colour option came with a green and white striped roof, all the others were fitted with a red and white striped roof. These were the points that Martin Walter used to promote the VW Dormobile on stand 86 at the 1961 Motor Show:

Touring for 7 with comfortable, face-forward seating for seven
Sleeping for 4 with patented 'Dormatic' seats convert to two 6ft beds, also two folding berths
Dining: folding table, built-in cooker, sink, water tanks
Headroom: 8ft 3in [2.5m] under elevating fibreglass roof
Storage: wardrobe, cupboard, two lockers

Engine: air-cooled, cannot boil or freeze. Easy starting. Rear mounting means excellent "bite" on all surfaces
Suspension: independent, all-round for smooth, level ride, better road-holding

Driving: car-type, all-synchromesh, 4-speed gearbox and extra manoeuvrability
Finish: 3 coats baked enamel for garage-like protection in the open

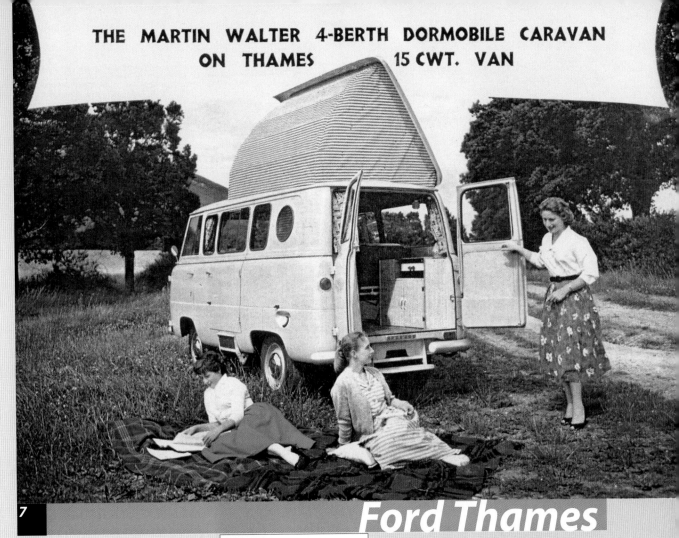

7

Ford Thames

The Thames 15cwt van by Ford is often the forgotten van in the history of light commercial vehicles in the United Kingdom; but, despite this, it was, in fact, hugely popular during the late 1950s and the early 1960s as a van and general utility vehicle. With few suitable base vehicles to choose from, the Ford Thames became an instant favourite with motor caravan converters, not least Martin Walter Ltd. They gave the Thames the full Dormobile treatment and launched the Ford Thames Dormobile at the Motor Show of 1958. By early 1959 the company's advertising department were working their magic, proclaiming that the Ford Thames Dormobile Caravan was a holiday hotel, restaurant car, beach chalet, four-berth sleeper, week-end cottage and six-seater tourer all in one. In the spring of 1959 you could have all this for the princely sum of £826, with no purchase tax.

For the design of the Thames Dormobile the team at Folkestone stuck to the successful formula that had proved so popular with their Bedford CA conversion. Once again, they fitted their side-

HOLIDAY HOTEL
RESTAURANT CAR
BEACH CHALET
4-BERTH SLEEPER
WEEK-END COTTAGE
6-SEATER TOURER

Yes...THEY'RE ALL INSIDE THE 4 BERTH

DORMOBILE CARAVAN

CONVERSION OF THE THAMES 15 CWT VAN

£826-10-0 NO P.T.

6 touring seats (which rearranged form 2 beds), 2 upper bunks, cooker, sink, table, cupboards and wardrobe are all included in the interior fittings of the Thames Dormobile Caravan. Ample roof height is achieved with an ingenious push-up roof canopy which is easily folded down to make the vehicle compact for travelling.

A money-saver on all holiday tours and week-end trips *and* for day-to-day use, the Thames Dormobile Caravan is proving a very popular buy indeed. And when you consider the many advantages plus the low initial cost—no wonder!

Full details from Ford dealers or the designers

Martin Walter Ltd
PIONEERS OF THE ALL-PURPOSE VEHICLE

Dept. A., UTILECON WORKS, FOLKESTONE
Phone Folkestone 51844   Established 1773
THE LARGEST PRODUCERS OF DUAL-PURPOSE BODYWORK IN THE WORLD

ABOVE: The Ford Thames range of light commercials was popular between 1957 and 1965. Martin Walter first used the Thames base for Dormobile Caravan conversion in 1959. This early sales brochure cover shows the Thames 15cwt van with the familiar rising roof.

LEFT: This Martin Walter advertisement for the Thames Dormobile was so typical of the period, emphasizing to potential customers that the Dormobile Caravan had many uses.

BELOW: This artist's impression of the Thames Dormobile Caravan shows the side door entrance, forward-facing rear seats and the storage pocket fitted inside the inner side door.

The Thames Dormobile camper has a great appeal, with attractive external lines and that Dormobile side body flash. When displayed at classic vehicle events (as seen here) the Thames always draws many admirers.

ABOVE: This delightful example was owned by Dormobile enthusiast Alan Kirtley, who has a habit of finding a good solid base and transforming it into an elegant showpiece. Distinguishing features on view here are once again the Dormobile side body flash, side door with air-scoop window, built-in lower entrance step and the neat porthole rear window.

LEFT: The interior of the Alan Kirtley Thames. Martin Walter used the trusted panel van layout on most of their rising roof models of the time, with cabinets at the rear.

hinged, rising roof with its distinctive candy-striped design and white GRP roof capping (but a roof canvas of plain fawn colour was an option). The large roof allowed for the fitting of two stretcher bunks, thus creating a four-berth model when these were coupled with the two single beds made up from the Dormatic seats. Martin Walter used the Thames van with twin rear doors and single side door, with the side entry door having a fold-away access step positioned on the lower side of the van.

The interior of the Thames had four single rear seats of the Dormatic design, and for travelling these were placed in the forward-facing position with a gangway in between. As an alternative, the rear seats could slide together to form a rear bench seat (remember that these were pre-seat-belt days). For night-time use the rear seats could be folded down to form two single, full-length beds, each measuring 72in by 23in (183cm × 58cm). With these beds in position there was still some standing room for dressing purposes, and access to the cupboards was not entirely restricted. In addition to the two lower beds, there were two stretcher-type bunks housed in the enormous roof space and access to these was by the usual, clever, little pull-out step, which folded away when not in use. The two bunks were designed to fold away neatly against the body sides at roof level. Each of the upper bunks measured 72in long and 21in in width (183cm × 53cm), and, to quote from the period publicity material, 'will accommodate a full 6ft tall person of corresponding weight' – make of that what you will.

On the Thames Dormobile models the units at the rear of the interior were constructed from wood with a limed oak Melamine veneer applied, as seen in the Bedford Romany and other campers. This material was used in order to present an attractive appearance and for ease of cleaning. For cooking, a two-burner hob/grill was installed, along with a plastic sink. Water was supplied on the early models via a gravity-fed tap housed in a unit on the rear nearside. Later models were fitted with the two plastic containers, held in place with straps at the rear of the interior. Gas for the cooker was held in a storage cradle under the floor in the centre of the camper. This area was capable of holding two gas cylinders or one cylinder plus additional storage space. An additional feature fitted as standard in the kitchen area was a folding stool; this was for the cook in the preparation of meals and for him or her to sit in front of the cooker.

With regard to the storage facilities, a wardrobe was situated on the nearside rear with hanging hooks. For food and utensil storage a cupboard was fitted beneath the hob and sink area. There was a further cupboard on the nearside for storing blankets and a locker on the offside of the interior for storing cutlery and crockery, the lid of which was intended as a 'useful tray'. Lighting was provided by two electric lights in the interior space, and on the early Thames Dormobile a further single gas light was also fitted. Curtains for all the windows ran on patented slide rails. It is surprising what the converters included in their sales publicity of the period; Martin Walter made a point of mentioning that the ash tray and front sun visors were standard equipment.

For dining, a table (with folding legs) was supplied to fit in the centre of the living area against the offside inner body of the vehicle. When not required, this was stored flat against the side of the vehicle. The usual host of optional extras was available for the Thames Dormobile from the comprehensive Martin Walter camping list. There was also a vast array of extras available from Ford at the time of ordering. As far as body colours were concerned, customers could choose from the standard Ford Thames range or from the 'Special' colours (and dual colour combinations) available from Martin Walter. The early Thames Dormobile models featured a plain 'factory finish' to the body styling, whereas the famous Dormobile side body flash (in contrasting colour) was later fitted. Martin Walter continued to market the Thames Dormobile up to the demise of the Thames range in 1965, when the Ford Transit was introduced.

This was how Martin Walter Ltd described the Thames Dormobile Caravan in December 1958:

One feature that Martin Walter Ltd carried through on all their Dormobile Caravan models comprised the distinguishing finishing touches. This close-up demonstrates just how the side body flashes were applied: aluminium sections fitted to the body and filled with colour inserts, chrome end plate and Dormobile lettering completing the finish.

Here is a Thames Dormobile Caravan in use at an unknown location during the 1960s. This must be an early basic model without a front roof luggage rack or side body flash.

Period publicity shot of the Thames Dormobile Caravan. A number of these models have survived in the hands of enthusiasts, which is commendable given that the last of them was built well over forty years ago.

Country Cottage on Wheels – introducing the latest Martin Walter conversion, the Thames 15cwt Dormobile Caravan, a single motorised unit combining car manoeuvrability with full caravan facilities, including cooker, sink, wardrobe and cupboards. There are six touring seats which can be arranged to form two beds: these, plus two upper bunks give total sleeping accommodation for four. A roomy interior height of 7ft 7in [2.31m] can be achieved by extending the push-up roof canopy which is also useful for a grandstand view at sporting events.

The purchase price for the Thames model at the end of 1958 was £874, and yet, strangely, the price stated in a period advertisement for April 1959 has the price set at £826 for exactly the same model.

BELOW LEFT: Interior publicity picture for the Thames Dormobile; note that the furniture had a habit of swapping sides. Also interesting here is that in those pre-computer days many photographs were coloured artificially.
BELOW: Yet another publicity picture, this time illustrating the interior of the Thames Dormobile arranged for dining.

The interior of the Ford Thames was quite narrow and therefore only two single beds could be formed from the Dormatic seats. Internal configurations were also hampered somewhat by the large engine cover/lid between the two front seats.

8

BMC J4

ABOVE: A new light commercial van from BMC for the 1960s, the Austin-Morris J4 was yet another forward-control design with the engine mounted between the front seats. As always when a new vehicle was released, Martin Walter were swift to turn their attentions to a Dormobile Caravan conversion. Seen here is one of the later versions from the early 1970s.

BELOW: Mike Cooke from north-east Britain owned this lovely example during the 1990s and attended classic vehicle shows and rallies all over the country.

The BMC J4 van, which came with either the Austin or the Morris badge, was to prove to be one of the most popular light commercial vans of the 1960s, and when it was introduced in 1961 Martin Walter quickly gave it the Dormobile camper make-over. Initially powered by the 1489cc engine, this was a forward-control vehicle with the engine mounted in the driving cab, between the two front seats. For their Dormobile Caravan conversion Martin Walter used the basic delivery van, without side door.

The company offered three variations on the J4: a 'Standard' two-berth (without rising roof), a 'De Luxe' two-berth with rising roof and a 'De Luxe' four-berth with rising roof. Prices within these options varied according to the paint scheme chosen; BMC standard colours were cheaper, with Martin Walter colour options available at a slightly higher cost. In fact, the practice of offering a standard or a de luxe model within the ranges of panel van conversions on a variety of base vehicles was quite common.

Internally the BMC J4 followed the standard Dormobile layout. This model

had twin-opening rear doors, and upon opening these the first noticeable feature was that the doors each had a storage pocket located halfway up, built into the door recess. The kitchen facilities were positioned to the left (when viewed from the rear), and these consisted of a two-burner hob with grill and a plastic sink beside it with a drainer. Both items had a lift-up lid hinged at the rear. It should be noted that the Standard two-berth models had a single gas ring in place of the two-burner hob. Another noticeable difference between the two- and the four-berth option was that the gas cylinder on the two-berth model was stored above the

floor of the vehicle, whereas the De Luxe models had the gas cylinders located in a special cradle beneath the floor. Situated under the cooker and the sink were storage cupboards behind sliding doors. A fabric waste bag in a candy stripe design was attached to the end of the kitchen unit via a turnbuckle fastener. Opposite the kitchen was a wardrobe, which contained a hanging hook and a vanity mirror. At the base of the wardrobe was fitted a pull-out step/stool, with the dual purpose of being a handy seat when the cooker was being used and a useful step for reaching the upper bunk beds in the rising roof. At the side of the

wardrobe (nearest rear of the vehicle) were the two plastic water containers, a large 5gal tank on a stand, fitted with a drain tap, and a smaller, 2gal tank above. On the other side of the wardrobe was an additional low-level storage box. All the furniture units in the vehicle were faced with a grey mahogany Melamine veneer, which was washable and hardwearing.

The seats were of the Dormatic variety, with the ingenious Martin Walter design, enabling them to be laid flat, folded up and turned around. The folding rear seats, in conjunction with the front driver and passenger seat, could be folded flat to form two single beds. The option of a double bed made up from these seats was not available on the J4 as the engine cowl restricted this. On the De Luxe four-berth models within the range, sleeping for a further two people was possible with the two stretcher-style bunks housed in the rising roof. An optional rear canvas annex/awning was available at extra cost and this had the capability of sleeping yet more. All the beds in the J4 Dormobile were at least 72in (183cm) in length, with the lower single beds being marginally wider than the upper bunks.

At meal times a table was provided as part of the standard equipment; this was erected to stand in the central gangway and folded flat for storage against the inside of the vehicle when not in use. For dining, the two rear seats were folded into the single bed position, forming two bench-type seats along either side. All the models had an electric light fitted in the front section of the interior, with the De Luxe models having an additional light for the upper bunks. Curtains for all windows were supplied as part of the standard package on all models in the J4 Dormobile range. The floor covering was of traditional lino, with aluminium edging for protection. All of the rear interior side walls were lined with a washable material, front seats were trimmed with a PVC material and the rear seats with a Duracour material. The J4 Dormobile benefited from good all-round vision for the occupants, with long side windows fitted in addition to those in the cab area and two single rear doors.

This is how Martin Walter Ltd set out the advantages of owning a BMC J4 Dormobile Caravan in their 1961 sales brochure:

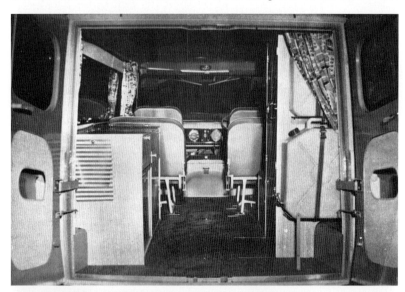

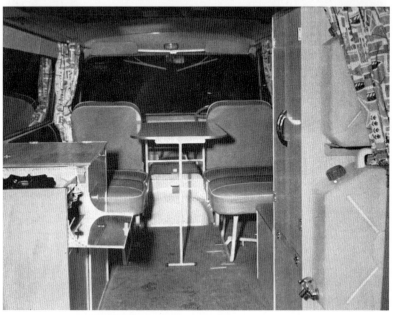

TOP: *No surprises for guessing that Martin Walter stayed with their trusted internal design for the BMC J4 conversion. It had already worked well on the Bedford CA, Standard Atlas, BMC J2, Ford Thames and early Commer.*

ABOVE: *The interior is seen again here, with the two rear seats folded down to create two bench seats for dining and the table erected in between.*

RIGHT: Early publicity shot of the BMC Dormobile Caravan as viewed from the side. The side body flash and Dormobile roof top will by now be familiar.

BELOW: Martin Walter Ltd had a habit of releasing this publicity picture with each new panel van conversion as a way of promoting their large rising roof with stretcher bunks. Being pre-computer days, the company actually made this roof demonstrator with a large section cut away.

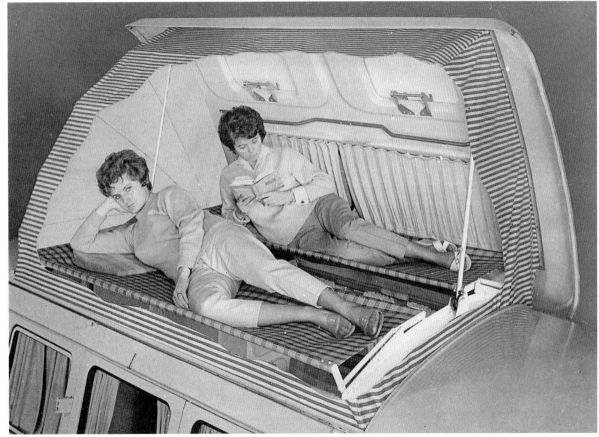

Wherever you go – You're at home with a DORMOBILE CARAVAN. The DORMOBILE Caravan is ideal for weekend picnic parties for the family. At race meetings and sporting events, it represents a mobile grandstand, with refreshment facilities laid on, and an excellent view is obtained through the large panoramic windows in the roof of the 'De Luxe' models, whatever the weather.

For travelling salesmen too, the DORMOBILE Caravan provides an office-cum-bedroom, saving time spent in looking for accommodation for the night in out-of-the-way places. The DORMOBILE Caravan can go wherever a car can go – further even; its excellent ground clearance and powerful engine are perfectly suited for off-road travel in search of seclusion – down narrow lanes, up mountain roads, it's all the same to the DORMOBILE Caravan.

Here's a newcomer to the fascinating Dormobile range. Its sparkling new conversion of the Austin 10/12cwt van and its keynote is a combination of space and comfort. It's all complete with beds for four and seats for six, plus an elevating canopy to give unrestricted movement. It has cooker, sink, wardrobe, a folding table and even the refinement of fluorescent lighting. Make this Dormobile your travelling home and day-to-day transport all in one!

Built-in gas cooker and sink units have ventilated cupboards under.

Hinged seat folds away or forms steps to upper berths. Glass fibre water containers show contents, have tap for easy use.

"Dormatic" seats swivel for use at table, or fold away, as does the table, to give clear floor area.

"Dormatic" seats form two single or one double bed. Two extra folding berths under elevating fibreglass roof on 4-berth models.

LEFT: This is how Martin Walter Ltd announced the arrival of the new BMC J4 Dormobile early in 1961. The price for a basic model started at £805, with a host of optional extras available.

RIGHT: Another advertisement from the period featuring the BMC J4. This one is also singing the praises of other Dormobile Caravans from the Martin Walter range.

Here is yet another piece of Martin Walter publicity, again it was issued for each new panel van conversion released, as was common to all Dormobile Caravans, with the exception of the VW.

The prices of the BMC Dormobile Caravan in spring 1961 were as follows: Standard two-berth model (no rising roof) £715 in colour from the BMC range or £725 finished in a colour from the Martin Walter catalogue. For the De Luxe two-berth model (with rising roof) the price was £805 in a BMC colour finish or £815 for a Martin Walter colour. The four-berth De Luxe, the flagship model in the J4 range, cost £820 for the BMC colour, and £820 for a Martin Walter colour option. As you might expect from Martin Walter, many optional extras were available for the BMC J4 Dormobile Caravan, from a front roof rack, to kitchen utensils, to vehicle fog lights and to camp beds for the optional rear annex.

9

Commer

ABOVE: This certainly is an early Commer Dormobile Caravan. The large Commer badge on the front, the lack of an air intake and three chrome strips denote this example as being a 1960–61 version. Once again the side body flash is evident.

RIGHT: The interior of the first Dormobile Caravan conversions on the Commer was quite different from that found on the later Commer Coaster. Needless to say, the familiar layout, as seen here, was again utilized.

Martin Walter Ltd produced their first conversion on the 1500 Commer chassis in 1960, to coincide with the release of the new vehicle from the Rootes group. However, this particular model was not then given the name Coaster, it was simply the Dormobile Caravan based on the Commer van, with side-loading door. This early model was typical Dormobile, featuring their well-tried Dormatic seating, the famous candy stripe rising roof and a wood grain plastic finish to the furniture. The Dormobile Commer Caravan had twin rear doors, which opened to reveal a cooker and sink unit on the right-hand side, with a spacious wardrobe to the left. Alongside the wardrobe were the 5gal and the 2gal water tanks fitted with taps. The seats for dining, which converted into a double bed, were situated just behind the cab area. This model was available as both a four- and a two-berth version, with stretcher bunks contained in the large Dormobile roof.

In 1969 the Dormobile Caravan on the Commer was re-released as the all-new Dormobile Coaster. In fact, several publications at this time quite erroneously proclaimed that this was the first Dormobile to be built on the Commer van. The Coaster was unveiled on the 'D Turner' stand at the 1969 COLEX (Camping and Outdoor Life and Travel Exhibition) show. D Turner was, in fact, Derek Turner, owner of the SE London Motorised Caravan Centre, a long established supplier of motor caravans in London and a well-respected supplier of all Dormobile models. The actual model then on display was the prototype Coaster. Externally it looked very similar to the model first released by the company in 1960; once again it was

The Commer reappeared as the Dormobile Coaster and one of the most obvious changes was the lack of the side flash along the body side. This is 'Duke' as owned by Scott and Bex with its delightful two-tone paintwork.

Despite the lack of a side body flash on this later Commer, the conversion was unmistakably Dormobile.

fitted with the Dormobile rising roof and, as before, it was based on the Commer van with side loading door. There was, however, one cosmetic change to the exterior bodywork of the new model: the famous Dormobile side flashing (a combination of aluminium trim running the length of the vehicle and infilled with a contrasting body colour) was missing on the new Coaster.

The interior of the new model bore little resemblance to that of the original Dormobile Commer. The designers this time had opted to lay out the interior in a similar fashion to that on many VW campers, with the bed to the rear and slightly to one side and all the furniture positioned along the interior side. The transverse bed on most Commer campers utilized the dinette seats, giving a bed length of exactly 6ft (183cm) across the van (as with models such as the Auto-Sleeper and the Car-Camper). By positioning the bed of the Coaster to the rear, Dormobile managed to add an extra 4in (10cm) to the bed length. There was, however, a price to pay for fitting the bed at the rear – it meant that no large items could be carried in the vehicle on a day-to-day basis when the vehicle was not being used for camping. For many people, the beauty of owning a panel van conversion is that it can be highly multi-functional and ideal as a back-up during house moves and when, for example, fetching large pieces of wood from the local DIY store. Placing the bed at the rear on a rear-engine van such as the VW appears quite logical, but to do this on a front-engine van with twin rear doors, such as the Commer, made, I believe, little commercial sense. But when used purely for camping, the Coaster layout was more than acceptable.

Running along the vehicle interior, directly behind the driver's seat, was the main Coaster furniture. This consisted of units at waist height housing the gas cooker (two-burner hob with grill), plastic sink, cool box (a refrigerator was an optional extra) and wardrobe. Fresh

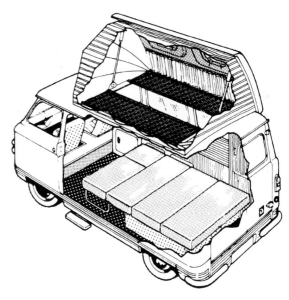

ABOVE: The majority of conversions on the Commer were carried out on the van. Dormobile utilized the version with side door access.

ABOVE RIGHT: This artist's cut-away drawing demonstrates the Dormobile Coaster arranged for sleeping. This was a four-berth model with the option of a child's bunk in the driving cab.

RIGHT: The interior of the Coaster was fitted with interior cabinets similar in style to those used in the VW D4/6, and laid out in a similar configuration. The wardrobe can be seen in the far corner and the bottle of chilled white wine looks inviting.

BOTTOM RIGHT: Alternative view of the Coaster interior looking toward the rear. The units consisted of the usual two-burner hob/grill with sink/drainer alongside.

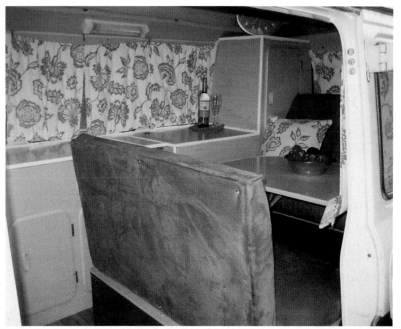

water was kept in a 3gal plastic container beneath the sink and transferred to the sink by a foot-operated pump. The provision for the storage of a gas cylinder was a box just inside the rear doors. Storage was a big plus point on the Coaster, with shelving under both the cooker and the sink. Below the drainer was a cutlery drawer. The rear wardrobe was of ample proportions and had a shallow shelf at the top. For the storage of bedding, there was more than enough room within the bench seat base.

The Coaster could seat four for dining and travelling; seven people could be seated in comfort. In addition to the rear double bed already mentioned, there were two stretcher bunks in the rising roof, and the driving compartment could be converted to sleep two children. Lighting was provided from fluorescent strip lights. Curtains were supplied as

LEFT: Another view of the Coaster interior units, which were all placed along the side, running from just behind the driver's seat to the rear corner.
RIGHT: A built-in cool box is visible here, with baskets. The lid was also insulated.

standard for all windows. The flooring was a combination first of vinyl and then a removable carpet. From its conception in the mid-1950s the huge Dormobile rising roof was one of the biggest fitted to any panel van conversion, and certainly one of the best. The GRP capping of this roof was fitted with two windows and a couple of opening air vents. To aid air circulation within the living area, two 'air scoop' Dormobile windows were incorporated into each side vehicle window. An interesting standard fitment on later models was a raised-roof warning light. This was a dash-mounted light that would illuminate when the ignition was switched on, should you be about to drive away with the roof still up.

The cost of a Dormobile Coaster in 1972 was £1,377 in standard form. The cost of the original Dormobile Caravan on the Commer base, back in 1960, was £908 for the four-berth model. A one-off, custom Dormobile Commer was created for RC Noyes of Surrey in 1964, a rather elegant, bespoke motorhome, but this was based on the Commer 1½-ton 'Walk-thru' chassis.

ABOVE: Interior of the Coaster with the beds in position; quite obviously a publicity picture from the bright and colourful 1970s.
RIGHT: A Dormobile Coaster in use at a camping rally during the late 1960s. The owner must have parked on uneven ground as the vehicle's lifting jack is being used for levelling purposes. I am sure that current Commer owners will find this amusing as the jacking points are often the first things to rot.

10

Land Rover

Matt Traxton of Northants is a keen Land Rover Dormobile enthusiast, having owned a couple of examples. Although he uses them for camping, he is not afraid to use them for the purpose for which they were designed – off-roading.

Alongside the early Volkswagen, the Dormobile conversion of the Land Rover remains one of the most sought after products from the range of Dormobile Caravans on the classic scene today. The Land Rover and VW conversions by Martin Walter also share another similarity – they were the only two Dormobile Caravans to be sold through Land Rover and Volkswagen dealers in North America. Based on the five-door, LWB (station wagon) chassis, the Land Rover 4 × 4 Dormobile was a 'go anywhere' utility vehicle in every sense of the expression. By the time Martin

Walter Ltd had added the vehicle to their Dormobile Caravan line-up the Land Rover was already a well proven, tried and tested design, renowned throughout the world for its no-nonsense simplicity, dependability and, not least, its ability to perform on the most rugged terrains and surfaces. For years before the release of this Martin Walter classic, people had been using the Land Rover as a base for camping, either by attaching canvas tents to the bodywork or installing their own makeshift camping facilities in the vehicle's interior. But, when the fully-fitted Dormobile

conversion arrived in 1961, it was a revelation to the many Land Rover enthusiasts around the world, because here at last was a purpose-built 4 × 4 camper, and not just any 4 × 4 caravan, this was a Dormobile fitted with their fully patented rising roof.

Martin Walter Ltd based the vast majority of their conversions on the LWB station wagon Series IIA option in the Land Rover range for the obvious reason of its internal space. However, I must point out that the Land Rover 109 three-door chassis was an option, but it would appear from the remaining

RIGHT: Martin Walter first introduced the Land Rover Dormobile Caravan in 1961; it became an instant success, despite being the most expensive Caravan they produced. Because of the Land Rover's rugged durability, it was much in demand around the world and proved to be a good export model. The example featured in these pictures is owned by Bill Bradford in Tennessee. It has undergone a complete rebuild and thus is in a fantastic condition. The Dormobile model was actually imported into the USA through Rover dealers in North America. They were in left-hand-drive format for that market.

BELOW: Side view of the five-door Dormobile Caravan on the Land Rover. Although the majority of these conversions did have the Dormobile rising roof, it was an option to have the roof fitted but with no camping interior, and, likewise, it was also possible to have a full camping interior without the rising roof. Martin Walter were also very accommodating if buyers had specific requirements for long-distance adventures.

BOTTOM: Camper vans of the 1960s did not get much tougher than this – all the attributes of a Dormobile Caravan housed within a go-anywhere vehicle.

records and surviving examples that few were ordered or built. The best selling and more popular five-door model allowed for full adult sleeping facilities, coupled with room for several pieces of useful furniture and, last but not least, the famous candy-stripe rising roof. The addition of that Dormobile roof had a habit of making most vehicles look better than they did in their standard form, and the Land Rover was no exception, the lines of the roof (both open and closed) complemented the base vehicle perfectly.

Two basic manufacturers' codes were used for Land Rover Dormobile models: the designation code LR626 was given to the more popular five-door LWB station wagon chassis, while the code LR625 was given to the two-door example, built on the 109 Land Rover. Both were available with either the 4- or the 6-cylinder engine, with a diesel unit available as an option at extra cost. Because Martin Walter offered the service of building a bespoke conversion upon any type of chassis supplied by a customer, it is believed that some Land Rovers were given the Dormobile treatment during the 1950s, although 'official' Land Rover Dormobile production took place between 1961 and 1975. For the purposes of describing the vehicle in this chapter I shall concentrate on the more popular model option, the LR626 version built on the LWB station wagon chassis.

One particular feature that was found in the majority of Dormobile Caravan conversions was the clever Dormatic seating, and the Land Rover conversion was no exception. These seats, which could be folded and turned into a variety of differing combinations, formed the base of this interior. The driver sat on a single Dormatic seat, which could be laid flat for sleeping; the passenger seat alongside this, again of the Dormatic design, was a double variety, but again with the option for it to be laid out flat. To the rear of these front seats were two singles, making a total of five forward-facing seats for driving. At night-time all of these seats could be folded flat to form two single beds or one large double. When dining the two rear seats were left in the forward-facing position, the double passenger seat was reversed to face the rear and the single driver's seat was laid flat, giving a total of five seats with the dining table in the centre. The traditional Dormobile table had folding legs and was stored against the side of the interior when not in use.

The large rising roof gave full standing height over the whole floor area behind the cab, this being the pram-type of rising roof incorporating two rectangular windows and an opening vent. Once again, Martin Walter Ltd had fitted a warning light on the dashboard in order to give the driver due notice that the roof was still in the raised position if he attempted to drive off. Housed in the roof space on the four-berth models were two stretcher bunks, which could be rolled up and stored against the sides when not in use. The Land Rover Dormobile had the traditional, one-piece, opening rear door, glazed at the top and hinged to one side. When this was opened, the two plastic water containers were to be found in the usual position, one on top of the other in the right-hand corner, the larger of the two being fitted with a drain tap. In the standard form, a wardrobe of good size was situated alongside the water containers, again with a hanging hook for clothes and a vanity mirror (I said in standard form because, if a refrigerator were ordered as an option, it occupied the wardrobe space). A pull/fold-out step/stool was built into the base of the wardrobe, intended as a stool for the cook and as a step to assist anyone climbing into the upper bunks in the roof space.

Opposite the wardrobe was the kitchen with a two-burner hob and grill, plastic sink and storage cupboards

LEFT: *Rear corner badges proudly display that this is a Land Rover Station Wagon. The maker's plate above this indicates that it is a genuine Dormobile conversion.*
BELOW: *A familiar sight to owners of 'series' Land Rovers, the spartan dashboard had basic instrumentation and a metal finish. The steering wheel on the left obviously identifies this as an export model.*

Interior view looking through the rear door, with Dormatic seats in the forward-facing position, rubber floor covering and stove-enamelled cabinets to each side.

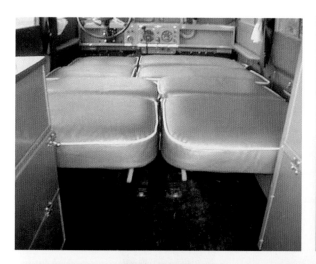

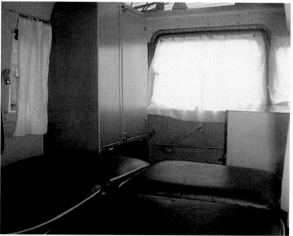

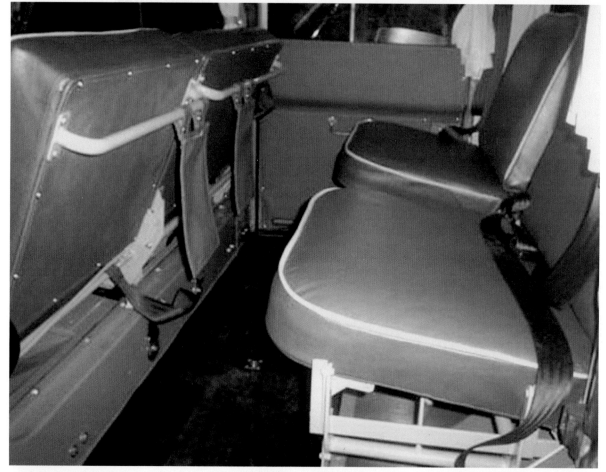

OPPOSITE PAGE:

TOP LEFT: *The famous Dormatic seats fold flat to form this double bed.*

TOP RIGHT: *The same bed layout looking toward the rear. There is still some empty floor space between the wardrobe and the kitchen for dressing and undressing, and for making a drink on the gas hob.*

MIDDLE: *This particular model has been restored to a very high standard, the interior looks as good as new. The two rear single seats can be seen here.*

BOTTOM LEFT: *The same view but lower down this time, clearly illustrating the mechanism on the base of the Dormatic seat.*

BOTTOM RIGHT: *Wardrobe in the corner of the interior, constructed from steel and stove-enamelled at the Folkestone factory. Clearly built for use and/or abuse, many examples were exported to Africa and North America.*

THIS PAGE:

TOP LEFT: *Alternative view of the metal wardrobe with twin opening doors and fold-out step/stool at the base.*

TOP RIGHT: *Would it be a Dormobile camper van without that folding step/stool? The idea first seen on the Bedford CA was carried through on all interiors, including the Land Rover.*

ABOVE RIGHT: *The facilities were basic yet functional inside the Land Rover – two-burner hob/grill with small sink alongside. Hinged lids folded back against the side windows and ample storage space was built into the cupboard below.*

RIGHT: *Simple yet functional best describes the cooking facilities: two-burner gas hob with grill beneath and a pull-down front flap complete the set-up.*

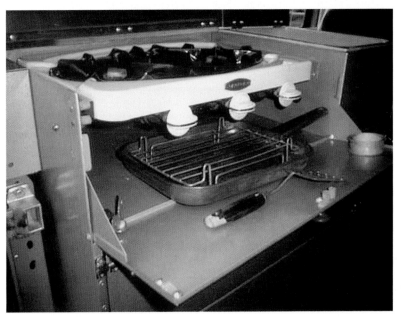

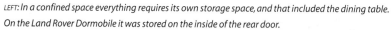

RIGHT: When dining, the table was erected by using folding legs and supported against the inside of the vehicle. Four people could quite easily fit around it using the Dormatic seating in varying ways; one option is shown here.

LEFT: No prizes for guessing what this is: the Dormobile roof in raised position and featuring the usual two windows and opening oblong vent. A pair of bunks were supplied, one of which is visible here, rolled up against the side.

below. A small shelf was fitted above the hob/sink to allow for extra storage. Both the hob and the sink had lids, which were hinged at the rear. Gas for supplying the hob was housed in the front of the vehicle, under the driver's seat, in a cradle. All the furniture in the Land Rover Dormobile was manufactured from stove-enamelled steel, with a 'hammered' paint finish in grey. The floor covering throughout was of a ribbed rubber design. In theory, these two combined factors were supposed to allow for the interior to be washed out after heavy use in muddy conditions.

Interior lighting was supplied by the standard interior light situated in the driving area and an additional fluorescent light on the edge of the roof aperture. Curtains came as part of the standard equipment to all windows. When it came to optional extras the world was

your oyster, the list of accessories available from Martin Walter was awesome. For the exterior of a new Land Rover Dormobile you could order anything from a roof rack to awning and a Dormobile tent to a portable shower. For the interior there were mosquito nets, a chemical toilet, food cabinet/cooler, fog lamps and a radio. In addition to these extras there was, of course, the whole Martin Walter camping catalogue to browse through, containing plenty of crockery, cutlery, saucepans and storage jars.

Because of the nature of the Land Rover it is highly likely that few Dormobile conversions were ever identical, such were the number of optional extras. It was possible to simply have the Dormobile roof fitted without any interior fittings, and likewise it was possible to have a complete Dormobile

interior without having the rising roof. Because many a Land Rover Dormobile was purchased for the express purpose of rugged off-road use overseas, the factory was very accommodating when it came to personal requests from customers. It was possible to have water and/or fuel can holders fitted to the exterior and holders for tools. The great majority of Land Rover Dormobile conversions were built on the Series IIA model, but some were built on the Series II, and some conversions can also be found on the Series III. Of course, now that the Dormobile name has been resurrected, it is possible to purchase a brand new model. It is widely accepted among Land Rover enthusiasts and historians that around a thousand plus Dormobile conversions were built between 1961 and 1975. When the 'all new' Range Rover was released at the end of the 1960s Dormobile were quick to offer the fitting of their famous rising roof to this model, with or without a camping interior. The Land Rover Dormobile could be ordered in either a right- or a left-hand-drive format.

As a price example, in February of 1962 a Land Rover Dormobile in standard form would have cost of the order of £1,198. The only competitor in the market place at that time was RJ Searle Ltd with their 'Carawagon' conversion of the Land Rover, and that was priced at £1,125.

11

Bedford CA Debonair

Released by Martin Walter Ltd in 1964, the Dormobile Debonair certainly took centre stage for innovative design and styling. In fact, the Debonair could not easily be classified – it was not a coach-built example in the traditional sense and neither was it a panel van conversion. The craftsmen at the Folkestone factory broke new ground by constructing a motor caravan using a one-piece, fibreglass-moulded model. Due to the long association the company had with Vauxhall Motors, the Debonair was available based only on the Bedford CA, 15/17cwt base. Only the small CA metal bonnet and grille section were retained, the remainder of the vehicle being a complete GRP moulding. The Debonair, released in 1964, continued in production on the Bedford CA until the introduction of the new Bedford CF in 1969. It was then restyled for the new base vehicle. For the purposes of this model description I am concentrating upon an example from 1966.

The Dormobile design team certainly brought all their years of experience to the fore when committing the

ABOVE: *The Dormobile Debonair was a radical departure from the normal camper vans built by Martin Walter. First unveiled in 1964, the Debonair based on the Bedford CA chassis was a complete fibreglass body, with the exception of the Bedford front grille section. This is an original press release picture from that period.*

The interior of the Debonair was certainly a clever design, as this publicity picture shows. The design team had managed to divide the interior into two by the use of the centrally placed kitchen.

Debonair to paper. This model had one of the most distinctive exteriors of any motor caravan from the classic period. The front end was distinctively Bedford CA. Just above the windscreen two separate, long windows were added for extra internal light and two further deep quadrant windows were placed to either side of the windscreen, giving the driver excellent views of the road, yet, at the same time, allowing even more light into the interior. At the rear of the vehicle were more beautifully shaped windows, letting light come flooding into the rear section. The GRP body afforded full standing height within the interior and two opening roof ventilators were fitted as standard. The interior of this model was neatly divided into two sections or 'cabins', as Dormobile referred to them. The forward area contained the cooker, an 'Easicool' food storage cabinet (or optional refrigerator) and forward-facing seats for five people. The rear cabin was fitted with lounge-type seating, which became the dinette when the table was erected.

On opening the one-piece rear door one was confronted by the lounge/dinette. Seating to each interior side of the vehicle had a textile covering, and a table (stored beneath a seat) could be erected with the aid of two metal legs and was placed between the seats for dining. The remainder of this cabin consisted of eye-level storage lockers, with yet more storage beneath the seat bases. The dinette seats converted at night into a double bed. All exterior surfaces in the dinette/lounge were finished in a wood veneer. Two wardrobes of a good size were also in this area of the vehicle, situated near the middle on each side. When viewed from the rear, a wardrobe could be seen on the left, next to a tall cupboard, which housed the toilet; there was a square louvre window mounted quite high in this cubicle. The forward cabin was a further seating area, also containing forward-facing seats for five (including the driver), and these seats converted into a second double bed. Easy access to the frontal area could be gained (in addition to the rear) via the passenger cab door. The kitchen in the Debonair was extremely well planned for such a confined space, with the possible exception of the refrigerator as this was situated in a slightly awkward position opposite the cooker in a narrow gap. The stainless steel sink was housed in the dividing cupboard, which separated the front and the rear area. Water was pumped to the sink via a foot-operated system and came from three 3gal containers. The containers were accessed by a floor well, the floor section being clipped to a bracket on the seat (a water heater was an optional

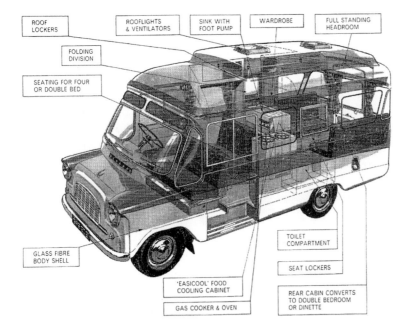

ROOF LOCKERS
ROOFLIGHTS & VENTILATORS
SINK WITH FOOT PUMP
WARDROBE
FULL STANDING HEADROOM
FOLDING DIVISION
SEATING FOR FOUR OR DOUBLE BED
GLASS FIBRE BODY SHELL
TOILET COMPARTMENT
SEAT LOCKERS
'EASICOOL' FOOD COOLING CABINET
GAS COOKER & OVEN
REAR CABIN CONVERTS TO DOUBLE BEDROOM OR DINETTE

ABOVE: This artist's cut-away drawing appeared in a variety of publications during the mid 1960s as a means of emphasizing all the Debonair features.

This is the view as seen from the passenger side door. The more popular four-berth model featured two bench seats in the front section, which, in true Martin Walter style, would fold flat to create a double bed. In the two-berth option the front bench seat was substituted for two single seats for driver and passenger. The water heater seen here fitted to the side wall in the centre was not fitted as part of the standard package and became an optional extra. A grey/yellow patterned Melamine finish was applied to all exterior cupboard fronts.

extra). Gas bottles were also housed in the floor, again a floor section being removed for access, and this was near the toilet/sink area. The cooker, with the oven, was placed near the toilet and the wardrobe, just behind the passenger seat. The cooker had a fold-up worktop and there was high, mounted storage cupboard above. Surfaces within the forward area were finished in a bright, hardwearing laminate. The Easicool storage cabinet (or optional refrigerator) was beneath the sink and accessed from the end. At this point I must mention the clever folding door/flap system employed by Dormobile on this model. The designers had not missed a trick on the Debonair and even came up with a simple way of dividing the front and the rear cabin by means of both the toilet door and other flaps. These were bolted into fittings to provide the Debonair interior with two completely separate areas, ideal for privacy.

During my research I found a recurring theme when reading the test reports on this model carried out over the years: each one mentioned the enormous amount of storage space that Dormobile had managed to fit into this unique motor caravan, given its dimensions. It was clearly designed by someone who had actually used a motor caravan, which, surprisingly, was not always the case with other conversions.

ABOVE: There were several colour scheme options for the Debonair, with the colour choice following this scheme, of Dormobile White as the main body colour. Martin Walter actually impregnated the colour into the fibreglass; it was not applied afterwards in the traditional fashion.
BELOW: This beautifully restored example has obviously had the body resprayed as the coloured pigment applied at the factory did fade after many years. This particular vehicle took a major prize at a classic camper van event.

LEFT: *The Debonair MkI on the CA chassis was produced in huge numbers at Folkestone, and thus a large number have survived; it also helps that the body was made from fibreglass as added protection against rot and rust. Patrick Osborne of Oxfordshire discovered this example sitting under a tree on someone's drive, where it appeared to have been parked for many years. He has since purchased the vehicle and is in the process of restoring it to its former glory.*

FAR LEFT: *Patrick's Debonair once more, this time the interior view through the single rear door. The rear section gave access to the kitchen facilities in the middle of the interior and was also the dining area when the table was erected between the two bench seats.*

LEFT: *The same view, but this time of the other side, showing the access to the front section at the end of the kitchen unit. The full-length wardrobe and toilet can be clearly seen on the left. The seats appear to be the originals in red Vynide with white piping.*

The view this time is through the driver's door (sliding window) across to the full cooker situated next to the wardrobe/toilet cupboards. The original bench seats can be seen, indicating that this was the four-berth model, more favoured by customers.

Patrick was fortunate to find the kitchen units in their original state as a number of examples from the 1960s have been chopped and changed by a succession of owners. There was certainly no lack of storage space in the Debonair.

Curtains were fitted as standard to all the windows on this model and fluorescent lighting was fitted to both the rear and the forward area. Martin Walter Ltd has always offered a bewildering array of options for all Dormobile models, and the Debonair was no exception. The basic options for the Bedford CA base vehicle were a four-speed gearbox (in place of the standard three-speed) and a diesel engine was an extra £125 from late 1966 to early 1967. Specific to this model was the option of a refrigerator in place of the Easicool cabinet at £45, a water heater at £35 and concertina-style blinds for the windows above the cab at £3.5s. The price listing for a Dormobile Debonair early in 1967 was £1,298 in basic/standard form. One interesting feature to note in relation to this model concerned the exterior colour: paint colours on the Debonair GRP body were bonded into the shell during its manufacture, a unique feature for this period. The standard Dormobile colours for the main body area

TOP RIGHT: Robin and Carole Phillips of London own this prize-winning Debonair, dating from the late 1960s.

RIGHT: This picture of their example clearly illustrates the amount of natural light that flowed into the vehicle from the abundance of front windows. The long triangular window gave excellent visibility when driving. The door glass was of the sliding design.

ABOVE: This is the obscure louvre window in the toilet compartment. The toilet area itself was no more than a crude chemical toilet, and, although popular at the time, many owners have replaced it with a modern counterpart.

RIGHT: The rear glazed corner section was a work of art, and again allowed plenty of light into the dining section.

were (in 1967) Dormobile White, Iris Blue, Foam Grey and Lime Green. The nose section, top coach line and vehicle side flash could be painted in any Martin Walter colour, of which there were many. As a point of reference, by far the most common colour combination for the Debonair was to have the main body in Dormobile White with the coach lines in a burgundy/red. The sales brochure of the period stated, 'repainting could be forgotten – the colour,

ABOVE: A good design feature of the MkI Debonair was the fold-down entrance step at the rear. A towbar with electrics has been fitted to this example so that one would have to take some degree of care, especially in the dark.

A rare factory picture, which illustrates the completed Debonair bodies awaiting fitments and the cleaning out of the window apertures. The Debonair bodies were actually cast in two sections (lengthways) and resin-bonded together.

Employees at Martin Walter Ltd fitting furniture inside the completed body shell. Here they are lifting the kitchen unit in through the rear door, with the cooker on the floor awaiting installation.

bonded into the material during manufacture, keeps its lustre'. I do not believe that Martin Walter Ltd thought for a moment that Debonair models would still be in use forty years later! Fading of the colours has now occurred on many surviving examples due to weathering, and thus repainting has had to be undertaken. The Bedford CA Dormobile Debonair was a great success story for the Folkestone company – it was hugely popular from the outset in 1964, received excellent press reviews and still remains a much sought after classic motor caravan.

When the Bedford CA finally ceased production and was replaced by the CF model in 1969 the Debonair name was carried over to the new model in the form of the 'Dormobile Debonair II'.

12

Roma

The little Dormobile Roma was a Bedford HA van, which was given the full Dormobile treatment, including a small version of the rising roof.

The Roma based on the Bedford HA van was certainly one of the smallest camper vans offered by the Folkestone factory; alongside their Ford Escort Elba, these were a pair of micro-campers in the Dormobile range. The diminutive Dormobile Roma was first unveiled at the 1967 Motor Show and caused quite a stir as this was the first car-derived camper to be offered by Martin Walter. Based on the Bedford HA 8cwt van and fitted with the 1159cc Vauxhall engine, the Roma was advertised as the camper van that would easily fit into the average garage. The design staff at Martin Walter did an excellent job of squeezing a quart into a pint pot, with the Roma having all the interior fittings of much larger models but in miniature. In one piece of period literature I discovered an interview with a member of the sales team at Martin Walter relating to the introduction of the Dormobile Roma. He stated that the number one target for sales of the Roma were, in fact, established motor-caravanners who already had a larger model and

might purchase the little Roma as their everyday car. But, as it happened, the Roma created a whole new market and introduced many newcomers to the joys of motor-caravanning.

'Drive small – park tall' was the slogan used to sell the Roma, and it certainly worked as sales within the first year exceeded expectations. This is how Martin Walter set about selling the Dormobile Roma in the motoring press (measurement conversions added):

> Our little Roma has given berths to a family of three – our little Roma stands 5ft 6in [168cm] on her wheels. She measures only 12½ft [380cm] long by 5ft [152cm] wide yet she can sleep you, your wife and child.
>
> With the roof raised and back extended, there's an extra 9½sq ft [0.9sq m] of floor space. Then you can unfold a 6ft [183cm] double bed out of the back seats. And pull down a 5ft 10in [178cm] bunk from the roof. (All your bedding, clothes and luggage will go in the three storage compartments.)

> Just so your family never wants for a wash or a hot snack, there's even a fold-away cooker and sink unit. For all her family ways, the Roma is still a lively, little Bedford 8cwt at heart. At the end of the day, she fits snugly in a 14ft [4.3m] garage!

The most distinguishing feature of the Roma was, of course, the rising roof, a scaled-down version of the same side-hinged design found on so many of the Dormobile camper vans. The roof was fitted over the whole of the Bedford roof area. As one have might expected, Dormatic seating formed the basis of the cleverly designed interior with the two front Bedford seats being retrimmed with material to match the folding rear double bench seat. An addition to the standard front seats was an occasional folding stool, which was attached to the back of the passenger seat; this was intended as a seat to aid the person using the small cooker. The rear bench seat was built on a tubular steel frame and a lever was pulled to enable the seat

to lie flat in order to form the double bed. But to do this, the design team decided to make the rear an extension of the interior by means of an enclosed section utilizing the vehicle tailgate. With the one-piece rear tailgate lifted up, two folding fibreglass panels then swung out to make the side walls of the rear extension. Double folding wooden panels then formed the extended floor, with a further wooden section (fitted with a cushion) taken from behind the rear seat and stood up on its folding legs in order to make the rear section of the double bed. As if this procedure were not complicated enough, another fibreglass panel was then removed from its cradle in the van roof and fitted to the side and end panels to form the completed extension. This gave an extra internal area measuring 3ft × 3ft (91cm × 91cm). It is not surprising to learn that Martin Walter Ltd decided to dispense with this design from 1969 and launched a MkII version of the Roma, which had a mini pram-type hood fitted as the rear extension, with material that matched that of the rising roof – an altogether better design, and which when in place complemented the little Bedford

ABOVE: This artist's cut-away drawing features the MkI model, which used GRP panels to form the rear bed extension. All the miniature interior fittings can be clearly seen.
BELOW: Factory photograph showing the production line for Dormobile Caravans. Two lines of Roma models are being completed here alongside the VW D4/6.

RIGHT: The MkII Roma was an altogether better design, certainly as far as the rear extension canopy was concerned.

The Dormobile Roma is an intriguing little box of tricks and always attracts a crowd at classic vehicle events today. A rather nice MkII example can be seen.

Things do not always go to plan at classic vehicle events, and snow was not forecast at this Easter weekend show! The Roma must have been rather cramped on this occasion.

far more than the cumbersome fibre-glass design of the MkI.

The main rising roof on the Roma was obviously a scaled down version of the full Dormobile roof, and to this end it contained only one stretcher bunk measuring 5ft 7in (170cm) in length and 1ft 7in (48cm) wide, and intended for a child. The bunk was rolled up when not in use and stored by the use of clips against the rising roof aperture. With the lower and the upper bunk in place it obviously required quite a strict routine to be adopted when using the limited amount of floor space.

Cooking in the Roma was by means of a very small 'Tilley' single-plate hob and grill, which would swivel out from the side of the vehicle and lock into place for use; this was positioned immediately behind the driver's seat. Beside the cooker was the small tip-up style sink, which when tipped up would drain the contents through a built-in hose, routed through the floor of the Roma. Beneath the hob and the sink was a storage cupboard with a single hinged door and above the kitchen was a useful shelf (level with the rising roof aperture). Water was carried in two 3gal plastic containers, one of which was housed under the dashboard (passenger side) and the other behind the driver's seat. A small water pump was fitted to the MkII Roma after complaints had been made about the cumbersome procedure for lifting these containers.

As one may imagine, the storage capacity inside the Roma was not vast. Apart from the kitchen cupboard already mentioned, there was a wardrobe to the nearside rear giving hanging space for a limited amount of clothing. Additional space was available in two cupboards just below roof level and to the rear (on either side of the rear bench seat). Two storage pockets were also built into the rear door. As the rising roof covered the entire roof of the Bedford, there was no room for a roof rack, with the result that any exterior annex/awning had to be carried in the vehicle when travelling. Curtains were supplied as standard to all windows and lighting was from a single electrical unit positioned above the kitchen area. The single gas cylinder used for cooking was stored in a recess in the rear, behind the bench seat. For dining, two very small tables were

ABOVE: The interior of the Roma was certainly compact and bijou. Occupants really did need to be on good terms as space was limited. The cooker and sink were quite tiny and the storage space was not designed with a long touring holiday in mind. The Roma was basically a weekend picnic vehicle, which was ideal for the occasional night away. It was sold on the principle that it would appeal to the one-car family who wanted a dual-purpose vehicle, which could also be kept in the average garage due to its size.

BELOW: The driving compartment of the Bedford HA Roma. Note the freshwater container in the passenger footwell.

The rear of the Roma featured a one-piece tailgate, hinged at the base. This is the MkII model as the MkI Roma tailgate was hinged at the top and lifted upward. The distinctive Dormobile side body flash can be seen here.

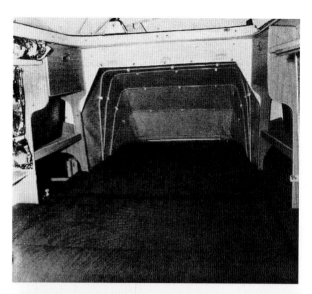

Looking toward the rear, with the MkII hood extension in place for sleeping.

Before the release of the Dormobile Roma, Martin Walter Ltd were, in fact, already using the Bedford HA van as a base for their 'Beagle' estate car, so the Roma design was a natural progression.

This is certainly a rare vehicle, a high-top version of the Dormobile Beagle estate car. It used to reside on the Isle of Wight but has not been seen for some time.

supplied, which clipped into a recess on either side of the rear bench seat.

Naturally a huge list of optional extras was available for the Roma owner, one of which was an extension tent giving valuable extra room when touring. A full list of camping accessories was available from the Martin Walter camping catalogue. The price of a Dormobile Roma MkII in the summer of 1969 was £825 for the three-berth De Luxe and £795 for the two-berth model.

Despite quite a large number of Roma models being produced between 1967 and the mid-1970s, it would appear that few good examples have survived the passage of time. There are certainly no more than a dozen in regular use in the United Kingdom. The Roma model was the last Dormobile camper to be fashioned by the famous Martin Walter designer Cecil Carte, who had been with the company since 1922, and it was his design team that had invented the brilliant Dormobile rising roof in the mid-1950s.

A fellow classic camper van enthusiast, Alan Kirtley, of Bedfordshire, has owned a variety of Dormobile models over the years, including a MkI Dormobile Roma, which he has restored and used. I asked Alan for his thoughts on the design of the pull-out rear extension on the MkI Roma:

I found that assembling the rear GRP canopy was a little awkward, it was certainly not as quick nor as easy as the later MkII Roma, with its drop-down tailgate and candy-stripe canopy, although it did make for a solid weatherproof enclosure, and certainly raised a few eyebrows on camp sites! The assembly involved first raising the tailgate and then unclipping the GRP panels, two of which then folded out from the rear of the camper to form the sides of the tailgate extension (as the roof). There was then a wooden panel which lifted out and formed the floor and another GRP panel which made up the end extension – this proudly wore the legend 'A Martin Walter Product'. One drawback with the GRP canopy extension was storage, it rattled when the camper was on the move and had to be packed with towels in between. Another point worth mentioning is that it was akin to sleeping in a coffin (or at least what I imagine that to be, having never tried it).

13 Land Cruiser
(BMC 250JU, Leyland 20 and Bedford CF)

ABOVE: Martin Walter Ltd first used the name 'Land Cruiser' for one of their Dormobile Caravan conversions in 1966, based on the Leyland 20 (formerly Standard Atlas). This was an adaptation of their current Dormobile Debonair GRP body, as seen on the Bedford CA, though this redesigned body for the Leyland chassis did not have all the windows to the front section and did not use a full GRP front section like the Debonair. The example shown here was a regular around the classic vehicle circuit during the 1990s but has now not been seen recently.

The Land Cruiser featured here is the version first offered by Martin Walter Ltd (Dormobile). I say this at the outset as there were models listed under the 'Landcruiser' name both in the late 1950s and again in the early 1960s. The Dormobile Land Cruiser was unveiled at the 1966 Earls Court Motor Show. When first released the motoring press picked up immediately on the fact that this new model bore a striking resemblance to the earlier Bedford CA Debonair body. But in fact the only real similarity between the two models was that the Land Cruiser was also constructed by using a one-piece GRP body. Unlike the Debonair, the Land Cruiser utilized the cab of the base vehicle, in

RIGHT: Robert Penman used to own this 1968 model. The Land Cruiser interior was unlike anything seen before on Dormobile Caravans, with cabinets and cupboards along each side and the dinette/double bed at the front, just behind the cab seats.

ABOVE: *The Land Cruiser based on the Leyland 20 was marketed by Martin Walter for only a couple of years, no doubt due to its poor sales. At the 1967 Motor Show another version of the Land Cruiser was launched, this time based on the new 250JU from BMC. This was a high-top panel van conversion and the name Land Cruiser had by this time been conflated into Landcruiser. Very little is known about this conversion as no sales brochures appear to have been released and no publications of the time carried out any road test reports. It is quite possible that it did not go into full-time production and that the show model was the only prototype produced.*

ABOVE RIGHT: *This is the more familiar Land Cruiser model based on the Bedford CF chassis; it was a further adaptation of the earlier body seen on the Leyland 20.*

RIGHT: *This excellent cut-away illustration shows the Land Cruiser interior in all its glory: four forward-facing seats and long bench-style seat/settee at the rear. The Land Cruiser was well equipped and included a rear corner toilet compartment.*

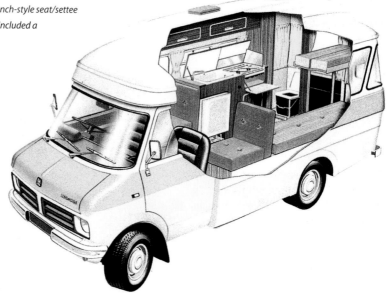

this case, the Leyland 20 (formerly the Standard Atlas).

The first Land Cruiser based on the Leyland 20 was not a great commercial success, but when the Bedford CF was released the Land Cruiser was reinvented, and suddenly Dormobile had yet another attractive model on their listing. The new Bedford-based Land Cruiser was first seen at COLEX (the Camping and Outdoor Leisure Exhibition) in 1971. Within a couple of years this model had become very popular. I shall therefore describe the Bedford version of the Land Cruiser, of about 1973. The Land Cruiser was based on the 22cwt CF chassis and was powered by the 2.3-litre petrol engine. This was another Dormobile model that had a one-piece GRP moulding, but retained the metal cab of the Bedford CF. The GRP moulding did, however, run the full length of the vehicle top, front to back with the low profile moulding over the driving cab also being of GRP material.

Entrance to the Land Cruiser was through a one-piece rear door, glazed at the top; access to the living area was also possible through the driving cab. Viewing the interior through the rear door, there was a toilet compartment in the right-hand corner, although the toilet itself was not supplied as standard. This compartment was fitted with a bi-fold door, which meant that the compartment could be extended slightly

when in use. The only drawback with this toilet compartment was that it had to double as the wardrobe. Situated next to this, on the same side, was the well-equipped kitchen area. It consisted of a two-burner hob with grill, storage units below and a sink alongside the cooker. A refrigerator was placed below the sink, which was a standard fitment on this model. Water was pumped electrically to the sink from a 12gal tank mounted

Derek Lancaster, a member of the Dormobile Owners Club, is the proud owner of this delightful example.

BELOW: The interior appears to be original, with the exception of a more modern refrigerator. There was full standing height in the Land Cruiser with an array of storage spaces.

under the floor of the vehicle. Eye-level storage lockers were situated over the kitchen unit, but these were not repeated on the opposite side.

Opposite the kitchen and toilet compartment was a long, well upholstered bench seat with matching backrest (the backrest was of a 'Pullman' type and assisted with the bed set-up), this ran to a point level with the end of the refrigerator on the opposite side. The dinette area was a piece of typical Dormobile ingenuity. In addition to the two seats in the driving cab, there were two forward-facing seats directly behind these. These two seats could be altered to form two inward-facing seats for dining purposes (bench style), with the addition of a laminate-topped table. With the seating arranged in this configuration, it meant that there was, in effect, a length of seating running from the rear of the vehicle to the rear of the cab passenger seat.

The sleeping arrangements once again made use of the dinette seating, kept in the dining configuration with the table forming the bed base; the back cushions were then placed over the table to complete a double bed. Bunk beds were quickly made up in the rear by utilizing the long seat opposite the kitchen. The Pullman-style backrest of

RIGHT: The interior as seen through the single rear door. To the left, and clearly visible, are the two 'cabin-style' bunk beds made up from the long seat/settee and metal supporting poles.

this seat could then swing up to form the upper bunk, with the assistance of two metal tubes; a detachable safety rail was supplied for the upper bunk as standard. This clever design meant that the floor space near the kitchen was clear and the toilet was still accessible throughout the night. There was the option of a stretcher bunk for a child within the cab area. The area above the driving cab was quite large and suitable for storing large items or bedding.

Additional features found in the Land Cruiser were a vanity mirror on the wardrobe door, lift-up roof ventilator, opening side and rear windows, ceiling-mounted fluorescent light, fully insulated GRP body, carpet to the cab area, vinyl flooring in the living area, curtains to all windows and provision for a gas bottle within a floor recess. The interior finish of cupboards in this model was a sapele-veneer effect laminate.

The Land Cruiser was a popular, well-equipped motor caravan and remains so on the classic scene today. Many examples have survived and are in regular use, both in the hands of dedicated enthusiasts and also simply as an inexpensive camper on the used market. The two main reasons for the wealth of surviving models are that it was built in substantial numbers and that the main body of the camper was constructed from fibreglass, and as a consequence, it did not suffer from rust problems like the traditional campers of steel construction. When the Land Cruiser was

The view from behind the passenger seat, looking toward the rear. The furniture finish was of the Melamine wood-effect pattern, with white plastic edging. Windows all round made for a light and airy interior.

This stunning example is owned by John Smith (another member of the Dormobile Owners Club). Period badge bar and whitewall tyres complement the exterior nicely. This is quite clearly a much cherished example.

ABOVE: This rear view of the John Smith Land Cruiser emphasizes the clean exterior lines of the design. The opening of the rear window at the top of the door was a neat design touch, allowing extra ventilation in the interior without having to have the rear door fully open. The entrance step is a later addition as the original would have folded down from inside a recess at the back.

RIGHT: The same vehicle, but this time the view is of the sink/drainer and cooker. The plastic sink and two-burner hob with grill were standard fitments, but a full oven could be ordered at extra cost.

first released in 1971 it was priced at £1,650 and by 1972 it had risen to £1,994. In the aftermath of the introduction of VAT in 1973 the Land Cruiser (along with all models) had risen in price considerably, and by 1975 the list price stood at £3,434.

But having already mentioned that the first Dormobile Land Cruiser appeared in 1966 based on the Leyland 20 chassis, I should also point out that before the release of the Bedford CF Land Cruiser, Martin Walter made another attempt to market the Land Cruiser name, this time on the BMC 250JU. This was a high-top panel van conversion with traditional Dormobile interior fittings. To date, I have only ever seen pictures of the original prototype model, which was displayed at the Motor Show; no road tests on this model appeared in the motoring publications of the time, and I have never seen a sales brochure for it.

Elba

ABOVE: The Ford Escort 'Elba' conversion; this is the publicity photograph released to the British press on 3 October 1968.

LEFT: Elba interior with the rear bench seat in the forward-facing position, arranged for dining at the two small side-tables. The very basic cooking facility can be seen on the left, with the sink unit opposite. The rear seat folded flat to make a double bed.

The Elba was released in 1968, based on the Ford Escort 8cwt van, and became a stablemate to the other Dormobile car-derived model, the Bedford HA Roma. Of these two models, it would be the Escort Elba that enjoyed the greater sales success, due in no small part to the popularity of the Ford Escort brand, which was available in saloon car, estate and van versions. Today, the MkI Ford Escort has a huge following on the classic scene in the United Kingdom, and the Escort Elba is always highly sought after. Again, it is a Dormobile model that was produced in quite large numbers, and some nice examples are still in use.

The appearance of the Ford Escort Elba marked a turning point in the history of Martin Walter Ltd. The company

called a press conference at a London hotel to unveil the two new models, the Elba and the Ford Transit Explorer. The press launch was entitled 'Dormobile Dormobiles', and the statement then handed out to those present went as follows:

A great number of people think they know what a Dormobile is, but in fact few are right. To settle a misconception, the manufacturers are taking the opportunity, at a time of major reorganization and development, to publicize the fact that 'Dormobile' is a registered trade name, applicable to the products of the Dormobile Division of Martin Walter Ltd.

Dormobile is therefore a brand; Dormobile stands for high quality and

outstanding design in a specialist field. Maintaining their lead in this field, Dormobile announce the introduction of two completely new, Ford-based motor caravans which will be on show to the public for the first time at the Earls Court Motor Show [of 1968].

This was a significant press conference in that it signalled the end of Martin Walter-produced Dormobile caravans and the beginning of a new 'Dormobile Ltd', although it was still part of the parent company.

The new Escort Elba Dormobile was unveiled amid fanfare and spotlights in London and the majority of the press corps there were impressed with it. But, on reflection, there was little new about the model except the Ford base vehicle – the Elba was simply the Roma carried over to another vehicle with a few tweaks and modifications. That is not meant to belittle the Escort Elba, which had considerable charm and thus was,

RIGHT: The double bed in position. The rear extension canopy hood can just be seen at the back.

BELOW RIGHT: Excellent line diagram showing all the features of the Dormobile Elba camper van. The top illustration shows the side view with rear canopy in place. The bottom view indicates the internal facilities.

BOTTOM RIGHT: Artist's cut-away illustration of the Dormobile Elba.

of course, quite appealing to established 'Ford' owners and buyers.

For the purposes of describing the vehicle I shall concentrate on the Dormobile Elba of 1972, as this was a mid-production date and probably marked the height of the model's popularity (pre-VAT introduction). The basis for the Elba was the Ford Escort 8cwt De Luxe van, powered by the 1.3-litre petrol engine as standard, although the 1100cc engine was available as an option. The Elba was built with full approval from Ford UK, with documentation carrying the 'Ford Approved Body Building' logo. As previously stated, the Elba was almost a carbon-copy of the Dormobile Roma first released in 1967. This was an occasional camper or picnic van rather than a fully fledged motor caravan, and, like the Roma, the Elba was once again a two-berth camper with the provision of a child's bunk in the rising roof. A full Dormobile rising roof covered the entire area of the Escort roofline and was fitted with a single opening roof vent and sealed rectangular window. The rear tailgate was a one-piece design, hinged at the bottom; this was folded down when on site and a canopy (matching the roof) was pulled down and fixed in place to complete the rear extension. Long windows were fitted to each side of the Elba body with each having an opening section built to Dormobile design. The standard Ford front seats were retained in the front driving cab, while in the rear a bench seat was installed of similar design to that found in the Roma. This would fold flat in order to be transformed into a double bed, utilizing the rear canopy area for sleeping. A folding stool was fixed to the back of the front passenger seat for use as an occasional seat for a third occupant and also for aiding the person sitting in front of the cooker.

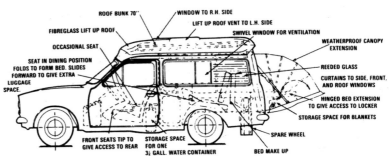

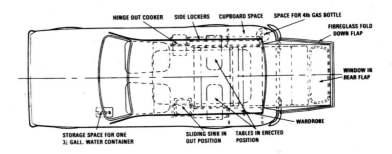

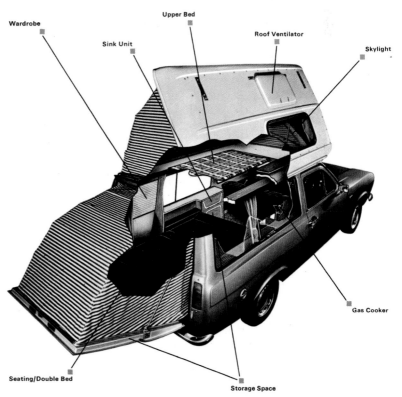

As in the Roma, the cooker was situated behind the driver's seat, on the side of the interior. In the standard form the cooker consisted of nothing more than a single Camping Gaz burner mounted on the top of a traditional Dormobile Melamine unit, with a storage cupboard below. A more conventional, single-burner hob with grill was only an option on the Elba model. At this point the interior design does differ from that in the Roma, because the small plastic sink was not situated beside the cooker but in its own small unit on the opposite side of the interior (behind the passenger's seat). This sink unit was of the tip-up variety with a waste hose connected and routed through the floor of the vehicle; a cupboard for storage was situated below. More storage areas, in the form of pockets, were built into the rear tailgate, and a small wardrobe was sited at the rear (on the same side as the sink). For dining, two small tables were provided, which attached to the sides of the vehicle (in line with the rear bench seat); these were stored within a special recess in the rear when not in use.

All the cupboard units in the Elba were the traditional Dormobile Melamine-faced plywood. Curtains were supplied as standard to all windows, and an interior light was fixed above the cooking area, together with a small storage shelf. A large vanity mirror was placed at an angle inside the rising roof. The mandatory flashing light would activate on the dashboard should the driver attempt to move with the roof in the raised position. The PVC/Terylene roof canopy was available in either a red/white or green/white combination.

The price of the Ford Escort Elba Dormobile early in 1972 was £1,118 in standard form. It probably goes without saying that there was the usual array of optional extras to choose from, both for the base vehicle by way of fog lights and a radio, through to the full Dormobile camping catalogue.

During my research I was fortunate enough to purchase a publication used by the Ford sales team in order to sell motor caravans. This not only informed the sales staff about the benefits of Ford-based camper vans but also looked at the competition. When dealing with the Escort they offered the Dormobile Roma as an example of the competition in the car-derived sector, thus:

> Bedford HA – the only competitor to the Escort in the small caravan class is the Dormobile Roma based on the original 1963 Bedford Viva van, and on pretty well every count it is an inferior vehicle, and, in particular, less suitable for use as a motor caravan.
>
> Shorter, narrower load space means less living space – in particular, the Escort can offer a longer roof bunk than the HA.
>
> Less power than the Escort (despite a recent increase to 1286cc) means poorer performance.
>
> More basic van-like trim.

It is more than a little interesting that the Ford sales staff would have been criticizing the Dormobile Roma to prospective buyers in favour of the Ford-based Elba. They also omitted to inform their own staff of another small camper in that sector of the market, the Suntor, by Torcars of Torrington, who had been having great success with their BMC A55/A60 conversion and were about to take the market by storm with their new Morris Marina Suntor.

LEFT: A number of Escort Elba models are still in use today, as the MkI Ford Escort has an enthusiastic following (in all forms) and parts remain quite plentiful.

BELOW: Close-up view of the rear extended canopy and the roof in the raised position.

The same vehicle, but this picture illustrates the difference between the Dormobile rising roof on the Elba and the 'straight up' design of the Torcars BMC model.

15 *Transit Explorer and Enterprise*

ABOVE LEFT: *Martin Walter Ltd quickly adapted the MkI Transit when it was released in 1965 and added the Transit Dormobile to their ever-growing list of models.*
ABOVE RIGHT: *This is an interior view of that first Dormobile Transit dating from 1966, a break with tradition this time as the designers came up with a complete fibreglass interior.*

EXPLORER

The Ford Transit Dormobile Explorer was unveiled at the same press conference as the Escort Elba model in 1968 and exhibited for the first time at that year's Motor Show. This was, however, not the first Dormobile conversion on the Ford Transit, since the company had released the 'Enterprise' camper a couple of years earlier. The Transit was released by Ford in 1965 and had quickly established itself as a popular base for conversion to camper van. Dormobile, as always, were ready to offer camper conversions on as many differing chassis as possible, and came up with an excellent interior layout for their new Transit Explorer in 1968.

The Explorer was based on the Transit 17cwt Custom van, with rear (single) tailgate and side access door, but later models gave the purchaser the option of the more traditional twin-opening doors. As this was a panel van conversion, it did, of course, feature the Dormobile rising roof, but this time a built-in luggage rack had been incorporated into the roof design. This was constructed from GRP and fitted to the front of the roof, with a slight extension that went over the front of the roof to form a peak. All in all, a very neat design, which complemented the exterior of the Explorer nicely.

This is how Dormobile described the Explorer in their 1969 sales brochure:

The homely appeal of wool moquette and wood-grained Melamine faced cabinetwork is here combined with the well appointed Ford Transit 17cwt custom version. The side access door incorporates an automatically retracting side step for still greater convenience.

Designed to seat up to seven, all forward-facing. This beautifully finished model is well equipped for any journey and includes such luxuries as fluorescent lighting, large ice box for food storage and a 6ft 4in [193cm] double bed! The bed may be made down independent of the front seats, to sleep two adults or four children whilst on the move.

Don't forget the Ford Dormobile Bonus! Free delivery (UK mainland), seat belts and a heater at no extra cost.

Those were the days when you were supposed to be grateful for free seat belts and a heater. It is difficult to understand what exactly Dormobile meant by 'or four children whilst on the move'; surely they were not advocating that children might be sleeping in bed while the vehicle was actually on the move? But I fear that that is what they did mean when one considers that seat belts were a selling point.

The Explorer's internal design had the main cabinetwork containing the cooker, sink, cool box and wardrobe all placed along the side of the vehicle, behind the driver's seat. The well-insulated cool box was, in fact, called a 'top-loading refrigerator' in sales literature after 1968. The cooker consisted of a two-burner hob with grill, immediately behind the driver's seat; the plastic sink was situated alongside it with a combined drainer. Next to this was the large, insulated cool box, with the wardrobe in the rear corner of the interior. All cabinets were faced with the familiar Dormobile wood-grained Melamine, with the cooker, sink and cool box having rear-hinged lids over them. The kitchen units also had storage space below for crockery and food, and the freshwater container was housed in the cupboard beneath the sink/drainer. Gas for cooking was supplied from a pair of cylinders stored under the rear bench seat.

At the rear of the Explorer was a ¾-width bench seat, sitting directly in line with the rear wheel arches. The brochures claimed that this seat would accommodate three people in the forward-facing position for travelling, when, in fact, two would have been far more comfortable. Immediately in front of this (in an omnibus layout) was another bench seat, which again would

Artist's line drawings are invaluable. This is one such for that early Dormobile Transit. This would later carry the model name 'Enterprise'.

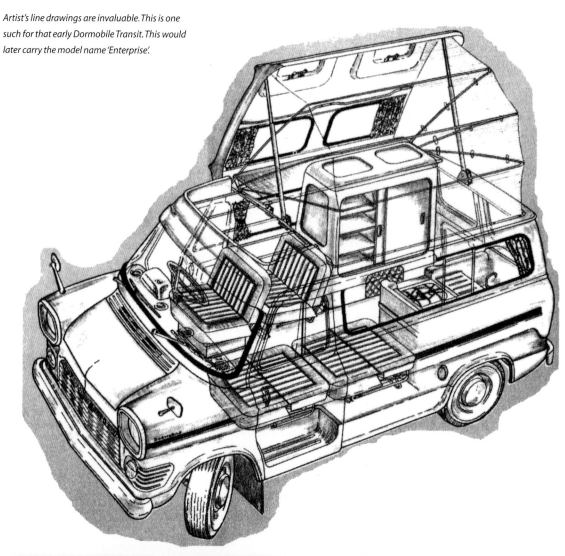

LEFT: *Rear interior corner of the Dormobile Explorer showing the GRP units that housed the sink and the cooker. The wardrobe is opposite, also constructed from GRP in a light grey finish.*

accommodate two for travelling. Underneath this seat was a locker box for storage and the dining table. It also contained a floor recess with cover – this was intended for the chemical toilet but was equally useful for a variety of storage purposes. Because this seat did not reach right across to the kitchen cupboard (for access purposes during the day), a seat/bed extension was supplied for night-time use in order to extend this seat across the width of the vehicle, in line with the rear seat/bed. Both this seat and the rear bench seat were used when dining, with the table erected in between.

The two rear bench seats used the Dormatic principle in order to form a double bed at night, with a further two bunk beds within the rising roof aperture, and the option of another bunk (stretcher type) across the driving cab area. To add the finishing touches to the Explorer it was supplied with curtains to all windows, fluorescent light in the centre of the vehicle and the warning device fitted to the rising roof to inform the driver that the roof was still raised should he attempt to move away. Other touches included a vanity mirror at eye level with the roof, and a removable carpet. As with all camper vans built in the Dormobile range, a full complement of optional extras were available for the Explorer, ranging from a gas oven with combined hob/grill in place of the standard two-burner hob/grill, Dormobile annexe/tent and, of

RIGHT: *The Dormobile Enterprise based on the Ford Transit and released in 1968. This side view of the MkI Transit shows the roof in the raised position and the built-in front luggage rack/visor.*

course, the camping extras in the Dormobile camping catalogue.

The price of an Explorer model in 1968 was £1,160.

ENTERPRISE

Released some two years before the Explorer but also based on the Ford Transit 17cwt Custom van, the Dormobile Enterprise looked similar to the Explorer externally. It did actually begin life simply as the Ford Transit Dormobile Caravan, but Dormobile saw the Ford Elba press launch as an opportunity to re-market their Transit model. The most noticeable difference between the Explorer and the Enterprise was that the latter did not have the side entry door. The Enterprise had the tried and trusted internal layout of the Bedford Romany, Thames and other panel van conversions from the Folkestone factory, with four single seats (Dormatic) at the front of the vehicle, which would fold flat to form two single or one double bed. Two stretcher bunks were housed in the rising roof.

Although the internal design of the Enterprise relied upon the tried and trusted Dormobile designs of the past, the construction methods used for the internal fittings were a radical departure from what had gone before. For the Enterprise, the designers had used a combination of fibreglass and plastic to create the sleek-looking cabinets. The company were masters of using this material, having released the fibreglass-bodied Debonair in 1964.

Although the construction method may have been ground-breaking, the cabinets were simply of the old design with a sink beside the two-burner hob/grill and with storage space below. On the opposite side was the very large wardrobe with the usual little step/stool built into the bottom. The remainder of

RIGHT: *Bird's-eye view of the sleeping/seating arrangements in the Dormobile Enterprise. The sleeping layout is on the right and the day-time layout on the left.*

RIGHT: *The Dormobile Enterprise based on the Ford Transit and released in 1968. This side view of the MkI Transit shows the roof in the raised position and the built-in front luggage rack/visor.*

The interior of the Enterprise, with this model being the complete opposite of the sister Transit the Explorer. For the Enterprise it was back to the trusted formula of Melamine-faced units and Dormatic seats.

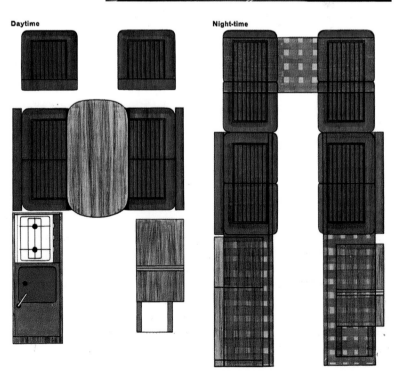

Daytime   Night-time

the vehicle featured all the usual Dormobile touches, such as curtains to all windows, a freshwater container, a folding table for dining and the addition, for this model, of a nice pair of GRP storage cupboards fixed to the inside of the rear doors. The price of an Enterprise in 1968 was £1,137.

Both the Explorer and the Enterprise failed to achieve high sales figures, despite the fact that they were well built and that they had the benefit of being based on the Ford Transit. As a result, Dormobile changed the interior design of the Enterprise, and out went the cabinets of GRP moulding to be

replaced with conventional wooden units. The Enterprise would undergo three changes in total from its original format and went from the MkI to the MkIII model before being deleted from the line-up. It would also utilize the Transit 90 Custom chassis during later production runs.

Fans of the Commer Coaster might just recognize this: the interior of the Explorer from a 1968 publicity picture.

Now Commer Coaster owners will be convinced: why build units for just one model when they can be adapted for others? This is the interior of the 1968 model Dormobile Explorer. The kitchen unit is displayed.

Bedford CF Debonair

If you are building a top-selling camper van and the base vehicle is dropped by the manufacturer, what do you do? In the case of Dormobile you simply switch that winning design over to another vehicle, and such was the case with the Debonair bodywork. The ground-breaking GRP body design of the Debonair was first seen in 1964 on the hugely popular Bedford CA chassis. The marriage between the Bedford and the Debonair design was a big hit with British buyers – here at last was a motor caravan body which would not leak with age, was light and had a spacious, well-designed interior. It was also mated to one of the most popular base vehicles of the period and, as a result, it sold in significant numbers. But in 1969 Vauxhall decided to drop the ageing CA model (in production since 1952) in favour of the CF model.

What happened next was quite remarkable as Vauxhall had given Dormobile some of the new CF chassis very early in production, the result being that

ABOVE: Another old name on a new model, this time the Bedford CF Debonair II. The roof and rear caravan body was a GRP moulding. This model would develop into the Dormobile Land Cruiser.
RIGHT: The MkII had a similar internal layout to the earlier Debonair on the CA chassis. The dining area is seen here at the rear of the vehicle.

Dormobile unveiled the new Debonair (and Romany) on the CF chassis before the 'new' CF range of light vans was officially launched. Although the new CF was different in every way from the earlier CA, there was little by way of change with regard to the Debonair, which was hardly surprising given the earlier model's popularity.

The MkII Debonair was based on the Bedford CF 106in wheelbase chassis and initially powered by the 1599cc petrol engine. From its launch, here is the

Dormobile description from one of their first MkII Debonair sales brochures:

The new Bedford Dormobile Debonair MkII is the ultimate in caravan luxury. Join the motor caravanning elite in the new Dormobile Debonair MkII – built for discerning families big or small, by craftsmen from Dormobile, the people who began it all. It is interesting to note that some big hire fleets make extensive use of Debonairs, a sure sign of its practicality and roadworthiness. There

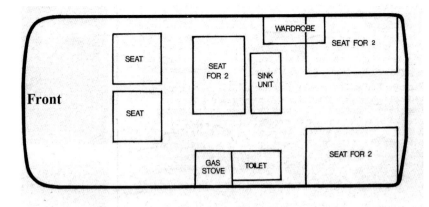

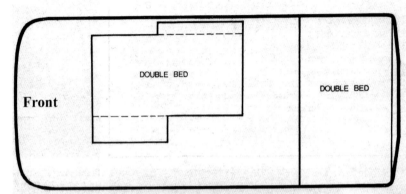

is a choice of eleven attractive Dormobile colours for the body side flash. All resin bonded moulding is in Dormobile white.

The Debonair MkI was the motor caravan perfectionist's dream. The new Debonair MkII is still that, and now the ultimate in luxury. The Debonair MkII is built to give years of reliable performance and caravanning pleasure. The new Debonair is exclusively for seekers after comfort – yet it seats as many as eight people in luxury! And what luxury – all upholstery is in a quilted nylon mixture fabric and stitched in nylon for sure! The body is constructed of colour-impregnated, reinforced moulded glass fibre, proof against corrosion, and its own garage all year through!

LEFT: *Floor plan for the Debonair II (four-berth).*
BELOW: *Rear of a Debonair II, although this one, seen at a classic vehicle show, has a slightly changed colour scheme.*

I shall not dwell in great detail on this particular Dormobile model since to a certain extent I would simply be reiterating what has already appeared in Chapter 11. The MkII version was almost a carbon copy of that first example, give or take a few dimensional differences and minor modifications. Suffice it to say that the MkII model was a well-equipped camper van for the period (1969). A major feature of the Debonair in both the MkI and the MkII format was the way in which the designers had split the internal space into two, ideal for a family with a couple of small children, since they could be put to bed in one half while the parents stayed up until later in the other; it was without doubt very well planned.

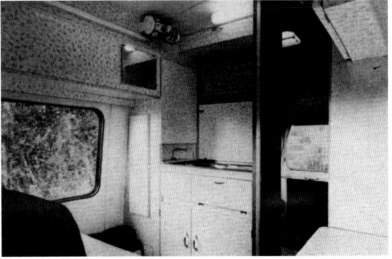

TOP: *Front view, this time with some retro body stripes added.*

ABOVE: *Interior of the Debonair II as seen from the passenger door.*

The Debonair MkII had seating for up to eight people; the rear used the two bench-style seats, which also acted as the dining area, with the addition of a table. The front of the vehicle had two single seats in the driving cab and a double bench seat immediately behind; the front and the back of the interior were divided by the centrally located kitchen unit containing cupboards and the sink. Other internal fitments included a cubicle housing the chemical toilet, a full cooker with oven beside it and a full-length wardrobe on the opposite side. A refrigerator or Easicool cabinet was available as an option.

Other standard features seen on the MkII Debonair included curtains for all the windows, water containers, fluorescent lighting, a vanity mirror, opening caravan windows and a rear step to aid entrance through the one-piece door.

The CF Debonair was produced alongside the Bedford CF Land Cruiser (similar body, different interior) for a while; late in 1971 a 4/5-berth Debonair would have cost around £1,994.

17 Bedford CF Romany

When the Bedford CF was unveiled in 1969, Dormobile had already announced the Romany II, such was the strong relationship between Vauxhall and Martin Walter Ltd. This is the Romany on its CF chassis. Externally there were only minor differences between this model and the later Freeway. The side windows are a give-away as two separate units were used on the Romany II sides.

As stated in the previous chapter, two camper van models made their debut on the 'new' Bedford CF before the CF range was officially launched – the Debonair MkII and this model, the Bedford CF Romany. This was yet another model name carried over from the CA to the CF, but, unlike the Debonair, Dormobile had taken the opportunity to make some significant changes to the new Romany. As with the previous Romany based on the CA Bedford, this was a panel van conversion with the Dormobile rising roof and rear entrance, twin-opening doors.

In this MkII Romany range were two models – a two- and a four-berth. The two-berth model was not fitted with a rising roof, but, apart from that, the interiors were exactly the same. The new MkII Romany did rely on the interior layout that had proved to be so successful on the long-running Bedford CA, with seats/beds toward the front and kitchen, sink and wardrobe at the rear. The most noticeable difference between this Romany and the earlier version was that the MkII had teak-finished furniture, available previously only on the upmarket Bedford CA Deauville.

The MkII Romany had four forward-facing single seats for travelling, and, as one would expect, they were of the famous Dormatic design with the ability to fold flat and form either two single beds or one large double. The seats were upholstered in Vynide material with a piped edging. In the rear of the Romany II was a large wardrobe on the driver's side, which had full-length hanging space and shelving, with more storage space at floor level. A traditional Dormobile trademark item was situated at the base of the wardrobe, the little fold-out step/stool. Opposite the wardrobe was the kitchen unit, consisting of a two-burner hob/grill with a coloured perspex sink and drainer alongside. Water was delivered to the sink by a foot-operated pump, with fresh water fed from two large containers. Beneath the cooker/sink was a storage cupboard and cutlery drawer.

The dining table, which was faced with Melamine on both sides, was located behind the wardrobe, with its removable legs stored beside the rear seats, along the side of the vehicle body. The gas supply for the hob came from a cylinder stored in a floor recess. A second underfloor container and chemical toilet were optional extras.

At night, the four single seats were folded flat to form two single beds; a double could be formed by using the backrests from the rear seats. Two further beds were located within the roof space on the four-berth model, and a child's bunk was an optional extra in the driving cab. The floor covering was linoleum (Cherry Red or Mist Grey), and a black rubber material covered the floor of the driving cab area. Other standard features in the MkII Romany included a fluorescent light in the living area (in addition to the standard cab light), a vanity mirror, insulation to the vehicle body sides and the usual safety device on the dashboard to alert the driver should he or she attempt to drive with the roof still raised.

The full complement of optional extras were available for the Romany II, which included an Easicool food storage cabinet, a child's bunk situated within the cab, a second recess in the floor for a chemical toilet, extra cavity insulation to the interior and a full complement of crockery for the kitchen cupboard. There are no prizes for guessing that the Dormobile camping catalogue was also thrust in the direction of Romany II buyers. This is how Dormobile Ltd sang the praises of the new Romany II in 1969:

> The new Mark II Romany is built on the brilliant new Bedford CF chassis and provides even more facilities than its illustrious predecessors. The new Bedford CF gives a spacious body, driver comfort, reliability, exceptional manoeuvrability and car-like performance with the high compression Victor engine. The Romany range gives a choice of extra roomy Motor Caravans designed for civilized and ordered living. Every model is designed and planned in detail, then craftsman-built for the maximum use of space. Efficiency is a feature of every fitment.

> • Dormobile elevating roof.
> • Fully sprung upholstered seats.
> • Dormatic mechanism making seats fold to give 6ft 4in × 5ft [193cm × 152cm] double bed, or 2 singles.
> • Teak finish to top-quality furniture.
> • Choice of 3- or 4-speed gearbox.
> • Choice from the super colourful new range of Dormobile colours to add a second body colour at a reasonable extra cost.

The Romany MkII based on the Bedford CF had a fairly short production run, and was replaced in the Dormobile line-up by the Freeway model, which, as well as being available on the CF, could also be purchased on the Ford Transit chassis.

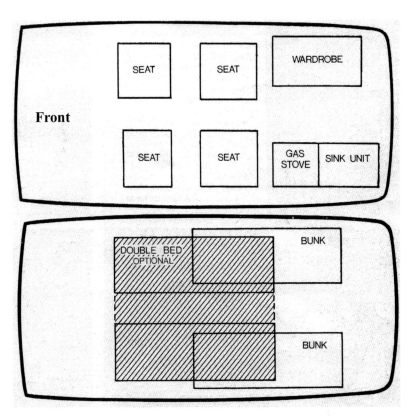

The floor plan for the Romany II; this will by now be a familiar Dormobile layout. The top diagram shows the day-time position of seats. The lower one shows the double bed in position and the two bunks in the rising roof.

The Dormatic seats in the Romany II were folded flat to create a spacious double bed, with two singles being an option.

Volkswagen D4/6

ABOVE: *Volkswagen Dormobile D4/6 fans will no doubt be envious of this beauty belonging to Stuart Burrows. This is certainly an early example of the classic Dormobile model, looking magnificent here with the roof raised and sun awning in place.*
LEFT: *View this time from the other side, showing the top of the famous roof, which in this case has been colour-coded with the vehicle.*

Throughout the 1960s the Dormobile conversion of the early VW had been in great demand, not only in the United Kingdom but throughout the world. The early VW Dormobile, with its distinctive rising roof, had also been available in North America through Volkswagen dealers, further enhancing the reputation of the Folkestone factory.

When the bay window T2 VW was released in 1968 it was also given a Dormobile camper make-over by the design team in Kent.

The D4/6 Dormobile Caravan was based on the Kombi (non-bulkhead), giving access between the driving cab and the rear. Like the previous VW Dormobile, the D4/6 used the famous side-hinged rising roof, but on this model they moved the roof forward slightly so that the roof aperture encompassed the front seat area. The reason given for this was so that the cooker could be placed in an unusual position, under the passenger seat. The repositioning of the roof therefore gave the cook the benefit of full standing height, but, in practice, the cooker was too low anyway and to use it with any degree of comfort the cook had either to sit on the driver's seat or, in fine weather, to stand outside. To quote from the accompanying sales brochure, 'Raise the front passenger seat for the best designed caravan cooker ever!' I am not sure whether

ABOVE: Stuart has opted to locate the spare wheel on the front panel of his VW, the other option being in the interior rear.

ABOVE RIGHT: The rear tailgate in the raised position reveals storage space above the engine bay and one of the cushions required to make up the double bed.

RIGHT: Another indication that this is an early bay model with the small rear lights. (Note the Dormobile emblem on the rear, perhaps that registration plate stands for 'very voluptuous bus'.)

they were trying to convince themselves or potential customers that this really was the best place for a cooker.

With the exception of the small wardrobe, all the furniture in the D4/6 was positioned along the side of the interior, immediately behind the driver's seat. It all had a wood-grain Melamine finish with white plastic trim edging around the doors and drawers. The furniture consisted of (from front to back) a plastic sink with drainer in a unit flush with the bottom of the side window, this unit was then stepped down and had a large, deep cool box. The sink/drainer and cool box had lids on their tops which were hinged at the back. Below the sink/drainer was a large amount of storage space in two cupboards (with hinged doors) and one cutlery drawer. Fresh water for the sink was delivered by a foot-operated pump at the base of the kitchen cupboard, with the water being stored in two

plastic containers housed in the base unit. A refrigerator was available as an optional extra and, if specified by the customer, it was housed in the kitchen base cupboard, leaving one storage cupboard with hinged door. A long, rectangular window was situated above the kitchen unit with a small storage shelf above it.

The wardrobe, a slim unit with a single hinged door, was immediately behind the passenger seat. The main seating area in the D4/6 consisted of a bench seat near the rear and two single 'buddy' seats. These seats were located just behind the two cab seats, facing

the rear bench seat. One of the seats was attached to clips on the edge of the wardrobe, while the other (again attached by clips) was in the access position between the cab and the living area. Both buddy seats were designed to be folded up when not in use and secured in place with a fastener. The dining table was attached to the side of the long kitchen unit, just below the cutlery drawer, and a combination of the bench seat and the two buddy seats allowed four people to sit at the table. The table was stored under the bench seat when not in use. The general storage areas in the Dormobile D4/6 were quite plentiful. In addition to the kitchen unit and the wardrobe there was also a small area behind the driver's seat and further storage in the rear, both behind the bench seat and above the engine. The spare wheel (with cover) was also housed in the rear corner of the interior, although some owners had this positioned on the front of the vehicle by using a suitable mounting bracket (though this was not a Dormobile option, according to my records, simply the personal choice of some owners).

Sleeping accommodation was provided by a double bed in the rear, utilizing the fold-flat bench seat, which was supported by the rear area and the erected table. This bed could accommodate either three small children or two adults. Two stretcher-style bunk beds were housed in the large roof void (5ft 11in (180cm) in length), with the option of another bunk bed across the driving cab area. If the two-berth option were purchased (without the rising roof) it was able to sleep two adults in the rear and one small(ish) child in the optional cab bunk. Of course, it was possible to sleep more people outside the vehicle within the optional awning attachment.

As part of the standard equipment Dormobile supplied curtains for all windows, interior fluorescent lighting, one gas cylinder, an interior vanity mirror and choice of carpet colour. The Dormobile D4/6 sold to the fleet market for hire purposes had the option of vinyl floor covering in lieu of carpeting, and Vynide covering to the seats in place of the standard tweed fabric. Using the Dormobile D4/6 specification guide for 1976, several options were available, which included a roof rack at £14.62, a child bunk in the cab at £26.91, a sun awning for £40.94, a 'Dormoloo' toilet £29.25 and a side tent/awning at £91.80, all quoted prices inclusive of VAT. The famous Dormobile roof canopy was supplied in either a red and white or a green and white colour combination, with exterior vehicle colours for the paintwork being available in single colour choices only, not two-tone. The price of a standard

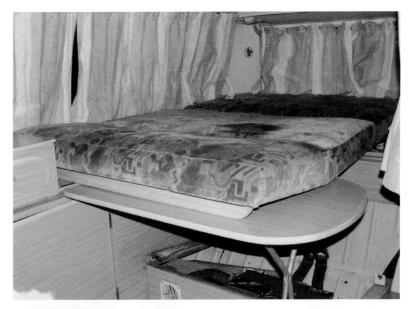

TOP LEFT: *Here is the double bed in position. The dining table is called upon to act as a support for it.*

ABOVE LEFT: *A more conventional use for a table perhaps, for dining and entertaining.*

LEFT: *Units in the VW D4/6 had the same finish as those in the Transit Enterprise and the Commer Coaster, Melamine-wood effect with white plastic edging. The small wardrobe can be seen on the left of the interior, slightly obscured by a green towel.*

Dormobile VW D4/6 in February 1976 was £3,609.88 (four-berth, with rising roof).

Today the Dormobile D4/6 remains a highly sought after model, both on the VW scene and among the devotees of classic camper vans throughout the world. It was produced in huge numbers at the Folkestone factory, and, as a consequence, a large number have survived the passage of time. My youngest son always vowed that when he was old enough he would buy a VW Dormobile as it was always his 'dream machine', and, sure enough, soon after passing his driving test an early bay model (1971) with that familiar Dormobile roof appeared on the driveway.

Today basic 'surf' or 'camping' vans are a common scene, mostly used by the young who take a basic delivery van (on a variety of chassis) and throw in a mattress and some camping equipment such as a portable cooker and a cool box. These vans are used for a variety of purposes from surfing, to mountain bike racing, canoeing, climbing and other outdoor activities. This sort of van-camping is by no means new, and one of the reasons why Martin Walter Ltd introduced the Utilicon van all those years ago. For those who wanted a dual-purpose vehicle in 1970s Britain, Dormobile released the Volkswagen D4/8, and, as the number designation suggests, it would carry eight and sleep four. The D4/8 was based on either the Kombi or the Microbus with side access door and would carry four in the forward-facing position. This model was available with or without the Dormobile rising roof. The interior did not feature any

fitted furniture and relied instead on portable units, which were stored in the rear (above the engine compartment). Options were available as for the VW D4/6, including a child's bunk bed across the cab.

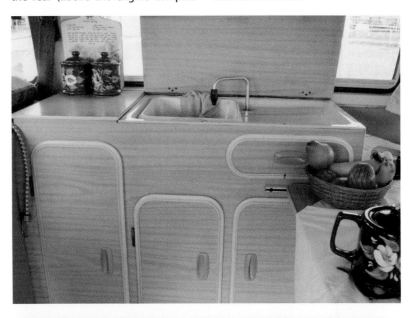

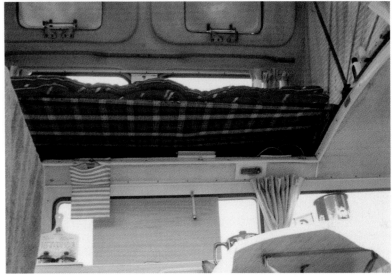

TOP RIGHT: A better view of the interior units with the plastic sink/drainer and storage cupboards below. The cutlery drawer is below the draining board and the metal support slot for the table edge can just be seen (near the fruit basket).

ABOVE RIGHT: Nice view looking up toward the inside of the rising roof. The tartan fabric of the stretcher bunk is visible here.

RIGHT: Some think it was a stroke of genius, others believe it to be madness, but this is where Dormobile decided to locate the cooker in the VW D4/6, under the passenger seat. Dormobile even moved the roof aperture further forward (than in the previous VW model) to accommodate this cooker. Seen here it looks ready for a veritable feast.

19   *Freeway*

ABOVE: The biggest selling Dormobile camper van of the early 1970s, this is the Freeway. It was available on the Bedford CF and the Ford Transit. This example, 'Little Red Devil', is owned by Alan and Cath Houchen of Leicestershire. The rising roof canvas has obviously been replaced at some stage, as plain red was not, I believe, a factory option.

BELOW: The same vehicle again, seen here with the roof closed. This picture illustrates the attractive external lines created by the GRP roof top and the front luggage rack/visor.

In this chapter I shall first focus upon the highly successful panel van conversion with the famous Dormobile rising roof, the Dormobile Freeway, and later I describe the Freeway model from 1973 based on the Ford Transit 90 van.

CF-BASED FREEWAY

This was a conversion of the Bedford CF 22cwt van from 1974 with a petrol engine fitted as standard and a diesel option available. This was a panel van conversion and so the side-hinged Dormobile roof was employed. Fitted slightly forward of the GRP roof capping was a contoured roof rack, again moulded in GRP. Entrance into the Freeway was through twin opening rear doors. Inside, one was confronted with a traditional panel van layout with furniture

TOP RIGHT: *Rear corner view shows the two-tone, red paintwork with the addition of modern graphics.*
BELOW RIGHT: *The interior of the 'Little Red Devil' Freeway. Twin-opening rear doors give access to the central gangway with units on each side. The dinette/double bed is just aft of the cab, with the bed in position in this picture; note the storage pockets built into the rear doors.*
BOTTOM RIGHT: *Alternative view of the Freeway interior with the dining table in position. The refrigerator, visible on the right of the picture, was an optional extra. Cabinets are of the Melamine-faced wood effect with white edging.*

positioned along each interior wall and the lounge/dinette just behind the driving compartment. These dinette seats (facing inward for dining) could be altered to give four forward-facing seats for travelling (although once again, in line with most panel van conversions of this period, no rear seat belts were fitted). The clever Dormobile seating configuration allowed for the two front seats, together with the rear ones, to become two single beds as an option to the double converted from the dinette. The spacious rising roof housed two stretcher bunks, both measuring 6ft (183cm) in length. A further option to accommodate another child for sleeping was in a stretcher bunk in the driving compartment.

Viewing the interior from the rear doors, there was a kitchen to the right-hand side. This consisted of a two-burner hob and grill, sink unit with water pumped from a 12gal underfloor tank, and several storage lockers and cupboards. The units were finished in a wood-grain Melamine. Split worktops on top of the sink and cooker hinged upward to act as splash backs. Opposite the kitchen was a wardrobe unit and next to this was either a dresser unit or the optional refrigerator (placed above either of these options was a large vanity mirror). Two further storage pockets were built on to the interior of the rear doors. Seating within the Freeway was finished in a nylon and tweed fabric and the floor covering was carpet laid over a Vynolay base. Even the cab area did not escape the Dormobile design touch, the dash being finished in a rosewood laminate. Curtains to all windows and fluorescent lighting complemented the rest of the interior.

LEFT: Yet another view of the interior, this time with one of the rear seats made up into the forward-facing position for travelling.

The Freeway was available in a large number of body colour options from the Dormobile range. There were a couple of special edition Freeway models released during production, one being the 'Pink Freeway' with a bright pink body colour, but if any now survive they have probably been repainted in a more conventional colour. Another special Freeway was the 'Tan Top' model. On this the GRP roof capping had a tan colour impregnated into it during manufacture (including the front roof rack). Furthermore, on this model the traditional red and white candy stripes on the roof fabric were changed to tan, brown and white stripes. Dormobile also offered a variation on the CF Freeway around this time entitled the 'Calypso'. Its roof was enlarged slightly and the tan, brown and white roof fabric was retained from the Tan Top special. The interior was also revamped with the kitchen and refrigerator switching sides. Other changes included a darker laminate finish to all surfaces and a distinctive flash decal to each side of the exterior. One of the most distinctive features of the Calypso was its tinted windows, designed to give the occupants more privacy. The cost of a Dormobile Bedford CF Freeway in 1974 would have been about £2,500.

ABOVE: The dinette area has a choice of layouts. The double bed is in position here, but the seats could also form bench seats on either side of the interior (for dining/relaxing) or two forward-facing seats for travelling.

ABOVE: Here is one of the seats behind the passenger seat in the travelling position. Other cushions, when not in use, were stored in the side pockets visible here.

RIGHT: The Freeway had the traditional Dormobile kitchen facilities of sink/drainer and two-burner hob with grill. A split worktop was hinged at the rear and folded back to make it possible to use the appliances.

RIGHT: The Dormobile Freeway was also available on the popular Ford Transit MkI. This cut-away illustration demonstrates clearly the model's attributes.

BELOW LEFT: The Freeway was an extremely popular model in the Dormobile range, consistently being the best seller. During its production run it underwent several minor alterations to the interior. This sales brochure front cover dates from 1973.

BELOW RIGHT: Dormobile made good use of the Freeway popularity by producing a couple of 'Limited Edition' models, the more popular of which was this 'Tan Top' model. For a period customers were also able to purchase a 'Pink Panther' special Freeway, with shocking pink paintwork and interior fabrics. Even the rising roof fabric was pink with black and white stripes. I know of no surviving examples and cannot imagine that it was ever in great demand at the time.

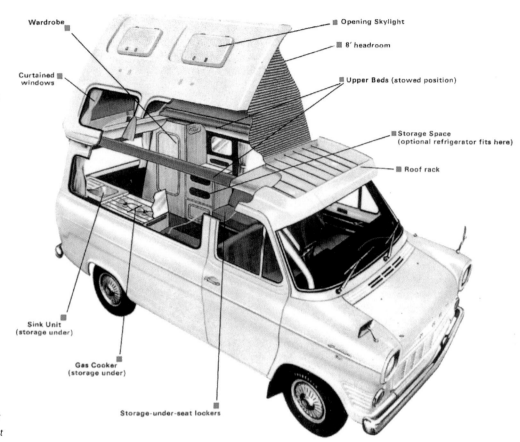

Wardrobe · Opening Skylight · Curtained windows · 8' headroom · Upper Beds (stowed position) · Storage Space (optional refrigerator fits here) · Roof rack · Sink Unit (storage under) · Gas Cooker (storage under) · Storage-under-seat lockers

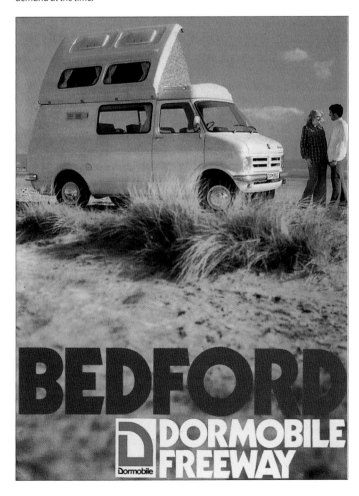

BEDFORD
DORMOBILE FREEWAY

New tan top Freeway

The roof, of course, is Dormobile's unique creation, and with the latest model — the Tan Top Freeway — this sleek roof design gets an exciting new touch of colour which transforms the Dormobile into a smart man-about-town vehicle when not in its holiday role.

ABOVE: Ford press picture of the 1974 Dormobile Freeway. Quite a number of Freeway models are still in use today on both the Bedford and the Transit MkI base vehicle.

BELOW: This picture from the 1970s shows three Dormobile Freeway models in line abreast at a camping rally.

FORD TRANSIT-BASED FREEWAY

Whereas the Freeway based on the Bedford CF had been a development of the earlier CF Romany, the Freeway based on the Ford Transit had evolved from the earlier Dormobile Transit models, the Enterprise and the Explorer. Both had been panel van conversions with a rising roof based on the popular Transit van. The Ford Transit Freeway itself was based on the Transit 90 chassis with the 1.7-litre petrol engine; a diesel option was not offered though automatic transmission was. The same roofline design principle was used on the Ford offering as had been seen on the CF Freeway. The side-hinged rising roof with a roof rack was incorporated into the front to form an attractive streamlined appearance. The red and white candy stripes on the roof fabric were evident here once again. Another similarity between the CF option and the Transit was the light Melamine finish to all the interior cupboards. The seating, dinette and sleeping configurations were also exactly the same as on the Transit model. The only major deviation came with the rear cupboard placement, and on the Transit the kitchen was moved to the right-hand side when viewed from the rear door. The wardrobe, vanity mirror and dresser/refrigerator were opposite. The majority of Transit Freeway models were based on the chassis with the one-piece, rear-lifting tailgate, as opposed to twin opening doors. The body colour was limited on the Transit to just white, red or primrose. The cost of a Dormobile Freeway on the Transit base about 1973 would have been around £2,500.

20

Dormobile built on a Fiat
Fiat 850

ABOVE: The little Fiat 850T was quite a popular base for conversion to a camper van during the 1970s, and, not to be left out, Dormobile joined in with their Dormobile Fiat D4/8 (sadly not a very original name).

RIGHT: The designation D4/8 signified that the Fiat would sleep four and seat eight. This advertisement must have been aimed at mothers on the school run in those pre-Chelsea tractor days.

Seats 8 (Adults/Children)

Given the long pedigree of the Dormobile name, which had been attached to camper vans since the 1950s, it was somewhat surprising that when Dormobile Ltd released a conversion on the little Fiat 850T they failed to give it a model name befitting their past glory. It was marketed simply as the 'Dormobile built on a Fiat', with the designation 'D2/8'. Enthusiasts of the Dormobile brand would argue that to attach the name 'Dormobile' was in itself enough to sell any camper van; but, as the 1970s began, competition in the camper van sector was becoming far more intense.

It is for this reason, I believe, that Dormobile should have given the quirky little Fiat conversion a name befitting its unique appeal in the 'micro-camper' sector, which was by then gaining in popularity. One should also consider that to design a very small camper van around the measurement constraints of the little Fiat must have been far more demanding than being given a larger interior such as that found on the Bedford CF or the Ford Transit. But the Dormobile

designers really did work their magic on the Fiat, once more having the ingenuity to squeeze a quart into a pint pot.

In the early 1970s the micro-camper sector was growing steadily in the United Kingdom, and already on sale in this category were such models as the Dormobile Roma and Elba, the Suntor, the Escort Siesta by Canterbury and other models on the little Fiat, such as the Fiesta and the Fargo. The sale of such vehicles was further enhanced by the fuel

TOP LEFT: *The Fiat featured a scaled-down version of the full Dormobile rising roof, seen here. In order to enjoy short breaks in the little Fiat the addition of a side awning/tent was highly recommended, in order to offer slightly more room.*

BELOW LEFT: *The Fiat 850T was a rear-engined vehicle, and thus a side access door was necessary. Dormobile used the same roof idea as seen on some of their other models – the built-in GRP luggage rack.*

BOTTOM LEFT: *It does not look like the most comfortable space in which four adults could relax without rubbing knees. If the gentleman in the spectacles wanted to use the toilet, I suspect that it would be a case of musical chairs for at least two of the other occupants.*

rationing in Britain. This is how Dormobile set out to advertise the Fiat Dormobile in their literature dating from September 1973:

The new way to travel for the family who know their way around. Yes, this unique new little Dormobile built on the amazing Fiat 903cc engined chassis opens up new ideas for family travelling. It can be used as a busy bee for nipping about from here to there or as a valuable workhorse carrying people and their belongings from place to place, however far apart.

A real hit for those who want the advantage of a really big-hearted estate and who at the same time envy the baby car drivers and their manoeuvrability. For holidays or picnics, for shopping, taking the young ones to school, for the retired or the young, for a silver anniversary or a wedding present, here's a new concept for the road by Dormobile.

No bigger than a small car, this Dormobile can comfortably seat no fewer than eight people. The envy of the school run brigade and a great shopping companion – on a really long session there's the facility and space for a sit down and a cup of tea. For moving furniture and the odd, really large parcel or piece of equipment this little Dormobile has plenty of room – don't let its outside measurements fool you!

The Fiat 900T was a rear-engined vehicle with access at the rear similar to that on the VW models, an engine inspection hatch at the bottom and a top-hinged opening panel above, with the

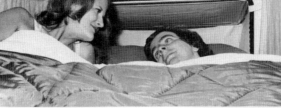

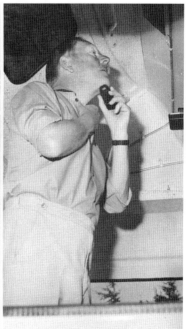

RIGHT: *This trio of publicity pictures does its best to sell the 'many' virtues of the Dormobile Fiat, including the opportunity to stand up and have a shave.*

BELOW: *The 'Carri-Galley' from Dormobile was the cooking facility in the Fiat model. With built-in water and gas supply, it could also be used outside the camper. It featured support legs and a carrying handle at each end.*

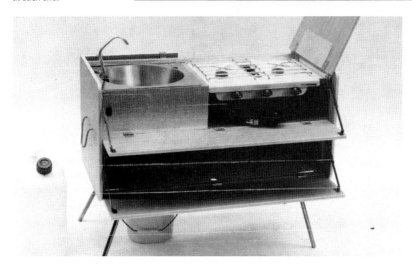

top-opening panel having a single rectangular window (non-opening). The driving position was similar to that of the Commer and the VW, with the driver and the passenger sitting over the front wheel arches. The Fiat had a slab-fronted design, once again akin to that of the Commer/VW. Entrance to the vehicle was by the driver and passenger front doors, and also a single side door. As this was a panel van conversion, Dormobile had fitted a rising roof; but because of size constraints on the Fiat, this was an adaptation of their more familiar design. Dormobile had fitted a GRP roof capping over the entire Fiat steel roof and within this had created an opening section for a 'miniature' Dormobile rising roof, with a luggage rack incorporated into the front section. For the rear end, Dormobile had used a design they had carried over

from their small Escort Elba and MkII Roma, a rear canopy with candy-stripe material. This worked by lifting the top rear tailgate and lowering the bottom engine inspection cover, the Dormobile extension was then fastened to these two tailgate sections.

The seating in the Fiat allowed for six forward-facing, of the bench style, and a further two-seater bench, which was rear-facing. Both the rear bench seat and the double bench seat aft of the cab would fold flat to create a double bed. This Fiat Dormobile was basically a two-berth with no provision for a bunk in the small rising roof. Further sleeping accommodation would have been available in the side awning/tent. Facilities inside the Fiat were basic: a table fitted in between the rear bench seat for dining, and storage comprised blanket storage under the rear seat. Further

storage was available under the central seat locker and there was a small hanging space for clothes situated behind the driver's seat. The fold-out canopy at the rear provided additional storage space when camping and was not part of the bedding arrangements as in the other Dormobile car-based models, the Roma and the Elba.

Cooking was done by means of a 'Bluet 200' hob, and a bowl was supplied for washing; both of these were stored in the central locker. As an alternative to the standard cooker supplied, customers could order a 'Carri-Galley' kitchen unit at extra cost. This was a fully portable unit consisting of a two-burner hob/grill and a stainless steel wash bowl with tap. The wooden unit had legs, a rear-hinged lid over the sink and a side-hinged lid over the cooker. It featured two drop-down sections at the front, and giving access to the grill and the other used for storage. The unit was completely portable, allowing it to be used outside the Fiat Dormobile.

As for the rest of the interior, curtains were supplied as standard to all windows, and a light was added to the interior living area. The Fiat Dormobile was available in several external body colours – olive green, white, blue and Monza red. The price of a Dormobile Fiat D2/8 in 1974 was £1,666. This compared favourably with that of other conversions on the Fiat at the time such as the Fargo, the Farina and the Huntsman.

21

Contessa

ABOVE: The Dormobile Contessa was aimed at the economy end of the camper van market. A Dormobile rising roof was fitted, but no built-in luggage rack on this model and only one window on the driver's side of the living area.

LEFT: Furniture in the Contessa was rather spartan, with thin plywood units, no lid over the sink, open storage areas and a simple camping gas stove.

The Dormobile Contessa was based on the Bedford CF 106in wheelbase van and marketed by Dormobile as the 'newest' idea in motor caravan design; this was how the company described the vehicle in their sales literature:

> The Bedford Dormobile Contessa is the newest idea in Motor Caravan design. It is a whole new concept in Motor Caravan marketing. It is very simple. The Dormobile Contessa is a soundly built, well designed model with all the essentials of a complete Dormobile Motor Caravan, and designed to appeal to the

individual who can personalize and improvise on the Contessa's profession-ally built foundation. For the lowest possible cost, the Contessa provides all the essentials in a basic layout.

In other words, it was a very basic camper van with minimal facilities, which was reflected in the price. The buyer could then do as much or as little to it as he wished in order to improve it. But that is exactly what buyers had been doing to motor caravans since the 1950s, no matter how much they had originally paid for the vehicle. Motor caravanners

have a tendency to add fixtures, fittings and accessories to suit their lifestyle and needs, they always have done and still do today. As a result, the Contessa was not a great sales success in comparison with other Dormobile models of the period.

The Contessa was the first Dormo-bile camper van for some time that was not fitted with Dormatic seating; this time the company had followed the design trend of fitting bench seats on either side of the vehicle, immediately behind the two cab seats. This tradi-tional seat/dinette design was at the time in use by most conversion special-ists. These seats were covered with a PVC 'button on' material, and this was obviously one of the areas where a buyer could improve on the original finish by fitting his own fabric. Because these seats were constructed on a wooden frame, it also meant that there was adequate storage below them, in large lockers; one of these housed the dining table when it was not in use. The table was placed in the gangway between these seats for dining, and the seats would easily fold flat to form a double bed. The Contessa retained the two standard Bedford seats in the driving cab.

Although promoted as an economy model, the Contessa was still fitted with the Dormobile rising roof, and, in line with the roof design, two bunk beds were housed in this area when the roof was erected. Once again a child's stretcher bunk was available as an optional extra for fitting across the cab, over the two seats. Internal cabinets were situated at the rear of the vehicle. On one side was a kitchen unit with plastic sink and drainer and ample storage facilities below. The standard two-burner and grill so often seen in Dormobile models was absent and instead of it a simple, 'camping style' gas hob, which had only two burners, was installed, this being a metal unit with a rear hinged lid. The kitchen unit was finished in a 'King Poly' faced oak, and presumably it was intended that a customer could either stain or paint these units in his or her own style and taste. The same could be said of the simple camping cooker since this would have been quite easy to upgrade, either to the more traditional hob/grill or a full cooker with oven below.

The large wardrobe was sited opposite the kitchen unit (and made from the same material) and was divided up internally with both hanging space for clothes and several shelves. A water container was housed on a high-level shelf next to the wardrobe and retained by a strap. A drain tap was fitted at the base of this container, and a further container was located in a recess at the base of the unit. Although advertised as an 'economy' model, the Contessa was quite well equipped and designed, curtains were fitted as standard to all windows and the floor was covered with vinyl.

Dormobile concluded their advertising for the Contessa with the following summary:

To sum up, the Contessa is a pleasing, well built, basic Motor Caravan that can

A view of the interior looking toward the rear: with two long bench seats folded flat to form a double bed, furniture at the far end, and a spacious wardrobe in the left rear.

The bench seats in the dinette area in their night-time position.

Dormobile proposed to the potential customers of the Contessa that they could take this basic camper van and improve upon it as they wished. In fact, that was what owners did, and still do, and, as such, the Contessa enjoyed only mediocre success. The table is seen in position here, supported by two metal poles sunk into recesses in the floor.

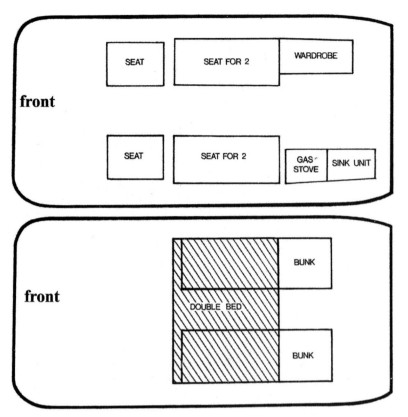

ABOVE: *Floor plan of the Dormobile Contessa.*

ABOVE: *The Contessa on display at the International Caravan and Camping Exhibition. The side of the Contessa was actually sign-written with publicity, the wording states – 'The Dormobile with the difference – the great idea from Dormobile – YOU MAKE the difference'.*

LEFT: *Dormobile had a habit of taking basic vans fitted with their rising roof and aiming them at a specialist market. This is the Dormobile Sportsman, the ideal utility vehicle for all outdoor types.*

become as luxurious, or remain as simple, as you wish. The New Bedford Dormobile Contessa is a new concept – see one and prove it for yourself.

The price for a standard Dormobile Contessa at the beginning of 1970 was held under the £1,000 mark at £998. By the following year the Contessa had been deleted from the Dormobile line-up when the Freeway was introduced.

The Contessa was by no means the end of the 'economy' models introduced by Dormobile on the Bedford CF chassis. Aiming specifically at the 'sporting' market, they introduced the 'Dormobile Sportsman', available as either the 1800 model or the 2300 Luxury. The words of Dormobile Ltd best sum up the vehicle:

Versatility is its speciality! Introducing an exciting new concept in town and country transport, the Dormobile Sportsman. Whether your interest is active (participating members of football, cricket, angling, water-sport, hunting/shooting/ fishing clubs and the like) or passive (spectator at outdoor events), the Sportsman is the ideal vehicle to use. Based on the Bedford CF, it's yet another example of Dormobile's unique flair for innovation. A truly versatile vehicle, with all-purpose/all weather appeal for lovers of outdoor living.

Thus, this was basically a Bedford CF Dormobile with a rising roof, built-in front luggage rack, but with a mini-bus interior in place of camper van fitments. The 1800 model was a thirteen-seater, with three forward-facing seats, and five-a-side benches, and powered by the 1.8-litre engine (hence the 1800 model designation). The 2300 model was equipped with six forward-facing seats, with space behind for six more passengers on fore-and-aft wood benches. As the model name suggests, it was powered by the 2.3-litre petrol engine. Because the Sportsman model had a rising roof and side windows, it did have the external looks of a camper van; as such, many were converted into campers by DIY enthusiasts in later years.

22

Calypso

ABOVE: The Dormobile Calypso carried a Caribbean theme throughout, both on the external paintwork and the brown, gold and white stripes on the rising roof material. But a more conventional colour scheme was available for customers requiring something rather less flamboyant.

RIGHT: The interior of the Calypso viewed through the rear doors, fashionable brown units throughout and brown upholstery material. No sign of any Dormatic seating here as the dinette seats were based on boxes with storage below.

The Dormobile Calypso was one of the more luxurious panel van conversions released from the Folkestone factory during the 1970s; this was an adaptation of the earlier Freeway model. The Calypso was based on either the Bedford CF 22 or the 250 van, with a high specification cab. The Calypso featured the Dormobile roof, though gone this time were the green/blue/red and white colour combinations for the roof fabric; this was now replaced by bold brown lines and contrasting gold and white stripes. This colour of the rising roof fabric had made an earlier appearance on the Tan Top Special Dormobile Freeway. Also missing from this model were the now familiar Dormatic seats, so often a part of Dormobile camper van designs.

The rear seats in the forward-facing arrangement for travelling. In this position a single seat base was retained behind each rear seat. The seats did, of course, fold flat to create two bench seats for dining with a table placed in between.

Seating in the Calypso featured raised boxes directly behind the cab seats; on these were upholstered cushions. These seats could be arranged to form two individual forward-facing seats for travelling (with two inward-facing seats). When camping these seats were folded flat to form a double bed and when dining the seats were arranged in two inward-facing bench seats, with a table placed in the central aisle. The table, with folding legs, was stored at the back of the wardrobe when not in use.

As with the majority of Dormobile panel van conversions to camper, the Calypso utilized the dinette seats to form a double bed measuring 72in by 42in (183cm × 107cm). The now familiar single stretcher bunk was again housed in the rising roof. A drive-away rear awning could be purchased as an optional extra, allowing more room for sleeping space if required.

As already noted, the Calypso was quite a luxurious model and comprehensively equipped as such. No plastic sink with drainer here, instead Dormobile fitted a combined stainless steel unit as standard. Water was housed in a container at the back of the sink/ cooker, and was transferred to the sink by an electrically-powered pump and could be refilled from the rear of the vehicle. There was the obligatory two-burner hob with grill, but this was also made from stainless steel, and an oven could be purchased at extra cost. The sink/drainer/hob combination was housed in a kitchen unit, with a good supply of cupboards and drawers beneath; this unit was faced with double-sided Melamine board in a chocolate brown colour to the doors and worktop, with the inner cabinet shell in a contrasting beige. The lid over the top

The Calypso was well equipped and included a combination sink/drainer and hob, all in stainless steel, with plenty of cupboard space below these facilities; the wardrobe and refrigerator were opposite.

of the sink and cooker was in two pieces, hinged lengthways along the centre in order to fold back neatly and act as a splash back. Opposite the kitchen was a centrally mounted refrigerator (at waist level off the floor), with a wardrobe fixed on either side. Again these units were finished in chocolate brown Melamine and contained ample clothes storage space for a family of four.

Other standard features of the Calypso included a vanity mirror with fluorescent light (inside the inner roof panel, at eye-level), curtains to all windows, felt-backed vinyl flooring and a water-level indicator gauge for the fresh water. A distinctive external feature of the Calypso models was the 'kick-up' (a Dormobile term) side flashes or graphics, in a contrasting colour to that of the main body. The main body colour choices for the Calypso were: Harvest Yellow, Aquamarine, Iris Blue, Foam Grey, Dormobile White, Diamond White, Ocean Blue and Honey Gold. The usual list of Dormobile extras was available, including a tow bar, child's bunk in the cab, vehicle underseal, gas cylinder and roof rack. One notable extra was the inclusion of Dormatic seats in place of the standard Bedford seats for an extra £129.60.

The Dormobile Calypso described here is the model dating from November 1978. The purchase price (inclusive of VAT) was £5,365.39.

ABOVE: And so to bed. The dining table was used to bridge the gap between the two side bench seats and extra cushions were placed between to form a double bed across the width of the vehicle.

BELOW: Interior plan of the Calypso. The top diagram shows the interior arranged for sleeping. The bottom diagram displays the interior in daytime mode.

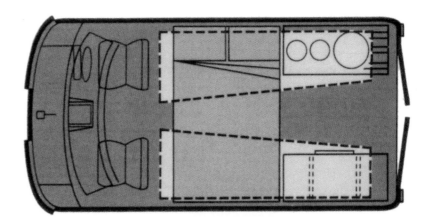

Layout showing the main double transverse bed and longitudinal roof bunks. An additional child's bunk can be erected in the cab compartment.

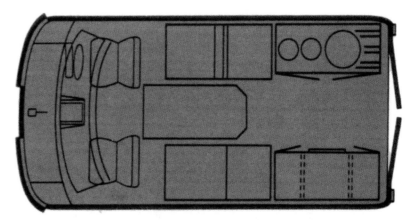

Layout showing the seating behind the driving compartment, which can be either two forward-facing and two inward-facing seats, or two inward-facing bench seats. The dining table position is also shown.

TOP: *The Dormobile Calypso in plain white paintwork at a caravan exhibition in the 1970s. In the foreground is the medal winning, Deauville coach-built example.*

ABOVE: *The 1979 Dormobile Calypso, once again in white with a contrasting colour for the body flash. The Calypso would prove to be the penultimate panel van conversion carried out by Dormobile.*

New World built on a TOYOTA
another WINNER

from Dormobile
Leaders in the Field...

23 *Toyota New World (coachbuilt)*

ABOVE: It was a brave attempt at a radical new design, but it failed miserably. The motor caravanning buyers were simply not ready for the Dormobile 'New World' based on the Toyota. As the cover of this brochure claims, 'another winner – sadly not, this one fell at the first fence.

New World production at the Folkestone factory, alongside ambulance conversions.

The coach-built Toyota New World model based on the Toyota was the first all-new coach-built to come out of Folkestone for many years, the previous model having been the Land Cruiser based on the 250JU chassis in 1966 (and later refitted to the Bedford CF). The New World was based on the Toyota Hi-ace chassis and was powered by the 1600cc petrol engine. Despite the fact that this model was in production for a couple of years, it would appear that the surviving examples have not stood the test of time – the early Hi-ace vans were notorious for rusting badly,

and one can only assume that of the relatively small number of New World models that were produced, the dreaded rust bug must have sent most of them to the great scrapyard in the sky, because, despite all my best efforts, I have been unable to trace a single Dormobile New World; in fact, the only one I have actually seen was a regular around the classic scene during the mid-1990s (in the United Kingdom), but even that has now disappeared.

The New World was a joint styling exercise between Dormobile and the famous staff at Ogle Design Ltd. This is how Dormobile described the New World in an introductory leaflet:

> What has been achieved is a highly stylized motor caravan of compact proportions that has a full specification to accommodate 2 to 4 adults. The outward appearance is of a well integrated body that is in complete harmony with the cab style and line.

The New World featured seating for three in the driving cab and six in the living area to the rear, with five of them forward-facing when travelling. The dinette area was directly behind the cab seats; this would seat four in comfort for dining and converted into a double bed. The rear of the vehicle had the kitchen in the far corner (driver's side), and this contained a sink (water pumped electrically from an underfloor tank), a two-burner hob and grill and a refrigerator as standard. The rear of the New World was a sealed design with no rear door access, but with a very large window that filled the top half of the rear section. Access to the camper from outside was through a door on the side, next to the passenger door. Opposite the kitchen unit/facilities was a large wardrobe, topped with a vanity unit complete with storage and a mirror. A door folded out from the wardrobe, right across the rear of the vehicle to form a private washroom/toilet.

All interior furniture was finished in Melamine-laminated sapele, with rounded edges for safety. There were plentiful storage cupboards and lockers in the New World. The floor covering was carpeting to the living area with rubber matting to the driving cab. There was a large perspex opening roof panel above

Toyota New World (coachbuilt)

ABOVE: *The shape of the Toyota New World was certainly an acquired taste. Note the huge, smoked glass panel above the windscreen.*

the kitchen, which extended rearward over the toilet/wash area. There was yet another large panel of this type above the windscreen, though this had a 'smoked' finish. One fluorescent light was fitted as standard, with a further two, small, courtesy lights.

Included in the price of £1,997 in 1972 were a spare wheel, tyre and tools, cab heater, radio, chrome front bumper (fender), refrigerator, carpet and a tank for fresh water. Available as optional extras were two upper bunk beds at £24, a sun awning at £23, the Dormobile 'family' tent at £76, a chemical toilet for £28 and retracting seat belts at £18.50 a pair. The only external body colours available were Dormobile White and Mid Grey.

ABOVE: *The rear design was slightly better with the large picture window. The New World was a side-entrance camper.*
BELOW: *New World survivors are a rare sight, this example was in use in the 1990s, based in Liverpool.*

BELOW: *Try as I might, I was unable to trace a New World model. The only interior shot I have is this rather poor press picture showing the rear of the interior.*

24

Dormobile Deauville (coachbuilt)

We finally arrive at the last coach-built model produced by Dormobile, the Deauville. This is the MkI example based on the Bedford CF 22cwt chassis.

The Dormobile Deauville first appeared in the early 1960s as an up-market model of the popular Bedford Dormobile Caravan based on the CA chassis. In place of the usual interior found in the standard model, Martin Walter had gone for a no-expenses-spared luxury interior, all built in wood by their in-house craftsmen. The company had taken the name Deauville from the fashionable coastal town in northern France, famous for its glamour and high society status. They believed (quite rightly) that the same could be said of their up-market Bedford Caravan, and the Deauville interior did gain rave reviews when it was released. When Bedford CA production came to a close in 1969, the Dormobile Deauville name was simply transferred to the new Bedford CF; but it must be said that the Deauville interior on the CF was not quite of the standard that it had been on the CA base. Out had gone the solid wooden interior to be replaced by

their wood-grain Melamine finish, and the CF Deauville interior closely resembled the interior layout of their Dormobile VW D4/6. The Deauville on the Bedford CF was a short-lived model, being in production for only a couple of years before it, and the Romany II, were replaced by the Dormobile Freeway in 1971.

Before commenting on the Dormobile Deauville coach-built model of the mid-1970s, I feel that it is important to summarize the state of play in the motor caravan market leading up to the release of the Deauville. Many companies in Britain were suffering by 1974 because of the three-day working week, power strikes and fuel rationing and the imposition of VAT in 1973, which had hit the leisure vehicle industry badly. As if these problems were not enough, the cost of base vehicles supplied to the motor caravan converters had also increased considerably. Many

of the small converters were able to ride the storm, but for the big companies such as the Dormobile Factory in Folkestone (with a large workforce and high overheads) it proved more difficult. As a result of all this, there were many redundancies at Dormobile, coupled with a cutback in production.

There were many in the industry at the time who were worried that Dormobile Ltd would not survive, and that may well have been the case had they not become part of the huge Charrington Group in 1973. The company set about restructuring for the future and also gained a new managing director, John Howell, who had been recruited from Caravans International. From this time on, the once market leaders in motor caravan production had to make sure that the future of the company was safe, and thus began a time of increased production of public service vehicles and small buses. Motor caravan production did not come to an abrupt end, the company was still producing a limited number of the Dormobile VW D4/6, the Bedford CF Land Cruiser and it reintroduced an old name the Romany, this time in MkIII guise. Sadly, the writing was on the wall as far as camper van production was concerned and only two more Dormobile Caravan models would be released – the coach-built Deauville and the Dormobile Toyota (with rising roof).

ABOVE: Another Deauville on the Bedford base, this time in glorious colour. Rather box-like in appearance, the Deauville was well equipped and featured an over-the-cab double bed, so popular at the time.

BELOW: Dave Hodgson of Dorset owns this MkII Deauville based on the Ford Transit. Dave has carried out some modifications to his Deauville, as owners of the older camper vans tend to do. It is seen here on a club rally in the French countryside.

BELOW RIGHT: *The dinette consisted of two bench seats to the side of the vehicle; this area converted into a double bed.*
BOTTOM RIGHT: *An alternative view of the dinette, clearly showing the shaped corners of the table to aid access to the seats.*

In 1977 the Dormobile Deauville was unveiled, an all-new, coach-built model based on the Bedford CF, Leyland Sherpa or the Ford Transit. The design followed the trend of the period in making a coach-built example by using sandwich-bonded material. This was constructed by using an aluminium outer skin, an extruded Styrofoam core and a plywood inner skin. This method simplified the initial build of the coach-built shell.

The MkI Deauville had a single rear entrance door, with this being glazed top and bottom, and a fixed entrance step with a non-slip tread applied. In the rear corner of the interior (passenger side) was the well-appointed kitchen containing an all-in-one stainless steel sink/drainer and cooker combination. The cooker had two burners and a grill, although a full oven below this could be ordered at extra cost; the top of the cooker/sink combination had a split worktop, hinged at the rear, with a folding metal flap to the side of the hob acting as a splash guard. Situated below the drainer was a refrigerator and there were storage lockers below this at floor level. If a gas oven were not stipulated below the cooker, then this became a further storage cupboard. The whole kitchen unit was faced with a wood-grain Melamine, reminiscent of medium oak in colour. Water was electrically pumped to the sink, and the Deauville was fitted with a 77-litre water tank as standard. To the side of the kitchen unit was another storage cupboard with a single door, built at a height slightly lower than the main kitchen unit, the top of which acted as a bedside table in the evening.

In the opposite corner of the interior was the washroom/toilet; this contained a hand basin and vanity cupboard (a chemical toilet at extra cost), and had a

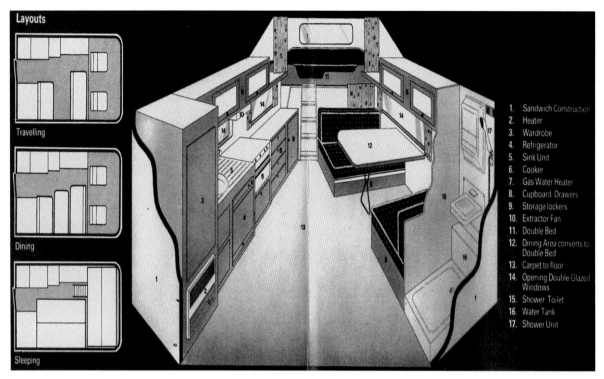

1. Sandwich Construction
2. Heater
3. Wardrobe
4. Refrigerator
5. Sink Unit
6. Cooker
7. Gas Water Heater
8. Cupboard Drawers
9. Storage lockers
10. Extractor Fan
11. Double Bed
12. Dining Area converts to Double Bed
13. Carpet to floor
14. Opening Double Glazed Windows
15. Shower Toilet
16. Water Tank
17. Shower Unit

Interior plan of the MkII Deauville Dormobile, a large, well-equipped motorhome with a high level of facilities.

small window placed quite high, just below roof level. For an extra cost a shower could be installed in the washroom, and a gas water boiler in the kitchen area to supply hot water. The outer door of the washroom was fitted with a large vanity mirror. Alongside the washroom was a wardrobe with hanging rail and shelving. A catalytic gas heater could be fitted at the base of the wardrobe at extra cost, but if this were not stipulated then this space was dedicated to storage. The finish of the washroom and wardrobe exterior matched that of the kitchen unit opposite. The floor area in the gangway between the washroom and the kitchen was finished in vinyl and edged with a metal strip, as the small area between it and the dinette was fitted with carpet.

The dinette area featured two inward-facing bench seats, well upholstered with thick foam and quality fabric material. These seats were built on to a wooden box frame, allowing for yet more storage underneath. A table was placed in the central aisle between these seats for dining, the table being of a similar finish to the furniture in the vehicle.

In its standard form the Deauville was a four-berth model, with the dinette converting to form one double bed; a further double was situated in the over-cab area of the large body. This high-level double bed was reached by a small ladder supplied; the area was lit from a long window at the top front of the vehicle. Lighting in the interior came from two fluorescent lamps above the dining area, a festoon lamp in the over-cab sleeping area, one light in the washroom/toilet and the standard vehicle light in the driving cab. Curtains were fitted as standard to all windows with the exception of the washroom. Gas bottle storage was in a cradle recess, which was accessed by a panel in the floor at the rear of the vehicle interior.

The model described here is the MkI Deauville. The MkII model had a much improved interior (with more cupboard space) with an altered internal layout. The coach-built Deauville MkI was priced at £6,367, based on the 2.3-litre Bedford CF in 1979. The model remained in production until the mid-1980s based on the Bedford, the Transit and the Sherpa; the only other model offered at the same time was the Calypso, also available on the same three base vehicles.

This Deauville based on the Bedford CF is sporting the standard factory colours. The Deauville was available on the Bedford CF, the Ford Transit and the Leyland Sherpa.

25

Dormobile Toyota *(rising roof)*

ABOVE: We reach the end of the Dormobile camper van story with this model, the Dormobile Toyota. After being the biggest producer of motor caravans in Britain for so many years, this was their only model on offer toward the end.

The saga of the Dormobile Caravan comes to an end. This chapter should tell the story of the final great camper van model to carry the famous Dormobile name, since surely the company had put all their decades of knowledge to good use by the early 1980s, but with the introduction of the Dormobile Toyota this was sadly not so. If anything, this particular model epitomized all that had gone wrong at the once great company, renowned throughout the world for its coach-building skills.

But before I describe the model I should explain my opening comment with regard to my disappointment over the Toyota Dormobile. Having studied the products of Martin Walter Ltd/Dormobile, both at first hand and through

This particular example dates from 1986 and was probably one of the final Dormobile camper vans to be built at the Folkestone factory. From this time until they closed down, Dormobile were only converting welfare coaches, buses and minibuses.

published material, I have come to appreciate their wonderful pedigree laid down over many years. It is upsetting that thirty plus years of motor caravan construction at the Folkestone

factory should end at this point, with a model of average interior quality put together with relatively cheap materials, since it did show. The design, however, was straight out of the top drawer

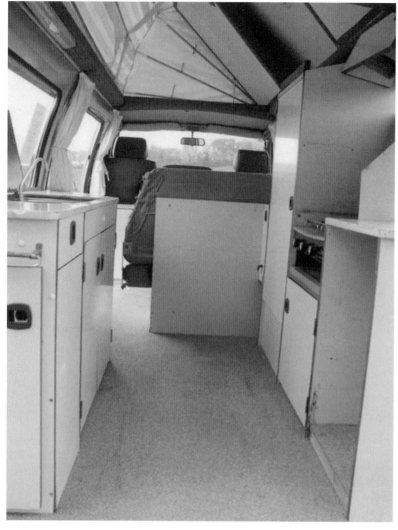

Apart from the rising roof, the Toyota is hardly recognizable as a Dormobile conversion, there were so few signs of the ingenuity and quality that had gone into previous models.

When I first saw this particular camper being offered for sale, I assumed that it must be a home-conversion. How wrong can you be? It was only the rising roof that made me investigate further. By Dormobile standards, the units were rather crude.

– as always from the team at Dormobile, they really had made good use of a limited space.

It was based on the Toyota Hi-ace window van (an excellent base vehicle) with top-hinged tailgate at the rear, and fitted with a modified version of the rising roof. This Toyota was a four-door van having two cab doors, a side access door and the rear tailgate (with glazed top half). It was a four-berth model, that is to say it would sleep two adults in the double bed at floor level and two more in the roof. The two stretcher bunks in the roof idea had long gone by this time and in their place was a double bed, which was made up by a selection of foam-covered boards that filled two-thirds of the roof area (leaving a gap for access). These boards could also be altered to allow twin beds to be positioned for children. The roof itself had been restyled for the Toyota, having slightly sharper edges and more of a slab-like look. Also missing now were the usual two small windows and the pair of opening vents. This roof had a single vent located in a central position. Externally, the roof was still pure Dormobile design, hinged from one side in a pram hood fashion, but the thin candy stripes on the material had given way to thick, bold lines of contrasting brown, white and gold, similar to the roof fabric of the later Calypso models.

The furniture in the Toyota was made from plastic-faced board and most of the units were positioned to the rear sides of the vehicle. The kitchen facilities had been split, with a stainless steel sink/drainer built into the top of one unit (passenger-side rear), with storage cupboards and a cutlery drawer. Water was pumped electrically to the sink from a container housed in a cupboard. The gas cylinder was also housed inside it and accessed through a door facing the rear. On the opposite side to the sink was a refrigerator at the rear end, this was inside a wooden unit with a worktop covering it. Alongside this was the two-burner hob and grill incorporating a lift-up lid; a single, side-hinged door below gave access to a storage cupboard. A special feature of the kitchen area was an electrically-operated ventilator fitted above the cooker and vented to the outside. A wardrobe of ample proportions completed the units on this side of the interior, with a four-bottle wine rack for good measure.

Seating in the Toyota allowed for three in the driving cab with two upholstered, bench-style seats in the rear living area. These were arranged in 'American diner style' (one rearward and one forward-facing) immediately behind the cab seats and off-set on the driver's side in order to allow access through the side door opposite. A table with a metal folding leg was placed in the middle of these two bench seats for dining, and attached on the interior wall by a patented locking system. The seat bases were of a generous size and therefore had quite a capacity for the storage of bedding and similar items. These two bench seats were folded flat in order to form the double bed, and the table was used to bridge the gap in between the seats. The left-hand corner of the bed had been shaped slightly in order to provide access to the facilities at the rear. To the side of the rearward-facing bench seat (against the bulkhead) was a small cabinet designed to be used as a bedside table when the double bed was set up.

Lighting came from two fluorescent units, one placed just above the sink and the other in the dinette area. There was also a small light fitted to the inside of the rising roof capping. The standard Toyota light fitting above the hob was retained. A modern addition to this

Some things never change, and even though this is a highly modified version of the original, it is unmistakably Dormobile. Gone though are the familiar bunks.

Dormobile was the fitting of a Zig distribution panel to the front edge of the left-hand unit. This provided an electrical supply to interior lights and charged the vehicle battery when mains electricity was available on campsites (via a suitable hook-up cable).

The finishing touches to the Toyota included curtains to all windows and entrance steps for the side access door and the rear tailgate section. With regard to the floor coverings, half of the interior was covered with fitted carpet and the remainder with vinyl. The exterior paint finish of the vehicle was that as supplied by Toyota from their colour chart, with no options given for any Dormobile colours.

The price of a Toyota Dormobile at the end of 1983 was £8,981. But by this time Dormobile had disappeared from all the motor caravan buyers' guides and was simply listed as offering conversions on the Toyota base vehicle.

Dinette area in the Toyota Dormobile. It did, of course, convert to a double bed, as all good Dormobile dinettes did over the years.

The company had been masters of the art of advertising their products since the early twentieth century, from carriages to cabriolets and everything in between (Martin Walter were still building carriages until 1922). Their products appeared in every trade journal and motoring publication, they were also regular exhibitors at the annual British Motor Show, gaining excellent reviews for their coach-building skills. This chapter is a pictorial revue of their products, mostly the famous Dormobile camper vans produced in their thousands from Folkestone.

Martin Walter Ltd placed advertisements for their Dormobile Caravan in just about every available publication, starting in the 1950s with magazines such as *Motor* and *Autocar*. Often those early attempts to put their message across to potential buyers would feature a photograph of a vehicle with a scene behind it drawn by an in-house artist. Many of the whole page advertisements were so visually appealing that today they stand out as an integral part of motoring history. Several of them that appeared on only a couple of occasions in a limited number of publications have become collectors' items. Of course, as a classic camper van enthusiast of many years standing, I was well aware that Martin Walter were prolific advertisers, but it was not until I began to work on this book that I became aware of just how much publicity material the company were responsible for.

It was enormous, but, due to the limitations on the length of the book, I can offer only a small selection in the following pages. It was a very pleasurable

chapter to compile, and I hope that you find as much interest in studying the advertisements as I had in finding them.

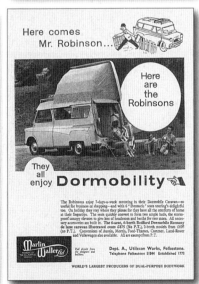

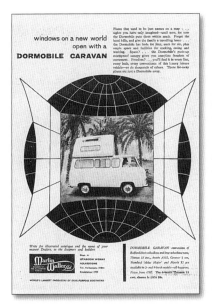

27

Dormobile time-line

a calendar of events

TOP: *The huge new Martin Walter factory on Tile Kiln Lane pictured in the mid-1950s.*
ABOVE: *The site today looks very different now that the old Dormobile factory has gone. The whole plot has now been divided up into small business sections, interspersed with service roads.*

1773 Martin Walter begins as harness makers.

1911 Martin Walter Ltd is formed, premises are purchased in Tontine Street, Folkestone.

1912 Managing director Spencer Apps opens a car showroom in Folkestone.

1921 Martin Walter Ltd display their coach-building skills at the Olympia show.

1928 The company displays a Bentley limousine at Olympia.

1929 Martin Walter builds the Speed Six Folkestone sports saloon.

1932 The company form closer ties with vehicle manufacturer Vauxhall.

1933 The Wingham Martin Walter first appears.

1935 The company registers the name 'Utilicon'.

1938–45 Martin Walter move equipment to a factory at Thames Ditton in order to produce munitions for the war effort.

1946 Martin Walter merge with the local firm Tapley Motors; Don Tapley becomes a director (the two companies had worked closely together before the merger).

1951 The idea of a 'bedroom on wheels' is developed and a prototype built.

1952 The Bedford CA launched by Vauxhall; the Dormobile 'bedroom on wheels' shown for the first time at the Commercial Vehicle Show and scores an immediate success.

1955 The success of the 'Dormobile' means that the old works on Cheriton Road, Folkestone are no longer large enough to cope with increased production; they are given the designation 'No.1' factory, and conversion of the Dormobile on the Bedford CA is moved to new premises on Tile Kiln Lane, Folkestone, and given the designation 'No.2' factory.

1956 Row upon row of Bedford CA vans are parked outside No.2 factory ready for conversion to Utilicons, Utilibrakes, Utilibuses, Workobuses, ambulances, mobile shops and Dormobiles; more than fifty vans a day are now passing through the factory conversion process.

ABOVE: The same site now, taken from a slightly different angle.

BELOW: Bob Brisley spent many years working at Martin Walter/Dormobile. Nowadays he is as a member of the Folkestone Camera Club.
Bob took this fabulous panoramic shot of the former Dormobile site on Tile Kiln Lane (and the other 'present today' photographs used here).

1957 A 'new' fully-fitted version of the Bedford CA Dormobile appears in *Autocar*; the Bedford Dormobile now has a rising roof, seats for four and a bed for two and is called the 'Dormobile Caravan'.

1959 Good news for Martin Walter as Vauxhall Motors announces modifications to the Bedford CA range; reports in the British press indicate that as many as eighty Dormobile Caravans a week are being produced in Folkestone; at the end of the year Martin Walter announce that they have converted 10,000 Bedford vans in a single year.

1960 With variations on different chassis, Martin Walter now has fifteen options within their Dormobile Caravan range.

1961 Land Rover and Volkswagen Dormobile campers are added to the model line-up.

1962 The BMC J2 and the Standard Atlas are dropped from the list of chassis used by Martin Walter for Dormobile Caravans.

1965 Under licence from Martin Walter Ltd, Split Level Safaris Inc. of Detroit build Dormobile Caravans on the Chevrolet Corvair and other chassis.

1966 Martin Walter announce a deal with Ford of Germany to import Ford Transit vans into Dover, convert them into Dormobile Caravans at the Folkestone factory and then send them back to Germany completed; strangely this was found to be cheaper than import-

ABOVE: The Martin Walter car showroom on Sandgate Road, with a pair of Bedford CA models on display. There were several of these showrooms in Kent for many years.

LEFT: The Martin Walter factory at Folkestone was producing so many conversions based on the Bedford CA that new vans were brought in by steam train. Seen here is the 'Dormobile Special' with yet another delivery.

ing the caravan components into Germany for assembly there.

1967 At the COLEX (Camping and Outdoor Life Exhibition) show Dormobile display a Bedford Romany, a Ford Transit and a prototype of their new hightop Land Cruiser based on the 250JU from BMC.

LEFT: The factory inspector (Vic Sayer) makes final checks on the completed vehicles awaiting delivery outside – a colourful sight.
BELOW: Martin Walter Ltd built their reputation for Dormobile Caravans on this model, the Bedford CA. This early example dates from 1958 and has been lovingly restored by Alan Kirtley.
BOTTOM: If Martin Walter were building all of those Dormobile Caravans, then someone had to sell them. Seen here was one of the main Dormobile dealers, D. Turner (Garages) Ltd of London. In this scene are a Dormobile Debonair on the far right, a Roma in the centre and a Romany (or Deauville) on the left.

RIGHT: *The Dormobile complex of buildings, as seen from the air.*
BELOW LEFT: *The high quality Deauville was introduced in 1962, an up-market version of the Bedford Dormobile Caravan.*
BELOW RIGHT: *Wilsons Motor Caravan Centre in London nearly always carried the full stock of Dormobile Caravans. This was the display outside the premises in 1964.*
BOTTOM: *The GRP-bodied Dormobile Debonair introduced in 1964.*

LEFT: The machinists inside the Martin Walter/Dormobile factory were kept busy producing the hoods for the famous rising roof.

BELOW: In any part of the United Kingdom during the summer months, you are never far away from at least one VW Dormobile Caravan.

Dormobile often exhibited a fine display of models at the annual Motor Show.

1969 The formation of two new companies; Dormobile Ltd becomes the new name for the manufacturing division, with D. Tapley as managing director; the world-famous Dormobile roof is symbolized in their new company emblem; the other company, Martin Walter (EKV) Ltd, then handles the distribution and sale of Vauxhall and Bedford cars and trucks in east Kent under the control of its newly appointed managing director Sir John Trelawny; news of a new Dormobile venture appears in the press; 'Dormobile Trailers (Ashford) Ltd' is announced; the new company is based at Martin Walter's former tyre sales depot at Ashford, Kent; it is proposed to build up to 4,000 trailer caravans a year by 1971; the Bedford CF is released to replace the CA range, and Dormobile models based on the new CF are announced before the official CF range launch by Vauxhall; in the spring Dormobile break new ground by launching a national television advertising campaign, mainly to promote the Volkswagen D4/6.

1970 Turners of London order £30,000's worth of Dormobile motor caravans from the Folkestone company; a press release states that Dormobile are to install a computer at their offices; Turners of London hold a one-week 'Holiday Show' at their premises to promote Dormobile models; Dormobile announce record production figures for the previous year of 1,969 camper vans on a variety of chassis; Alan Hopper, formerly of the sales department for camper vans, is appointed sales manager of Dormobile Trailers (Ashford) Ltd.

1971 Three new models this year from Dormobile: the Bedford Land Cruiser, the Freeway and the fitting of its famous rising roof to the luxury Range Rover 4 × 4.

1972 Huge sales success for the Dormobile Freeway models as it is announced that £373,000 worth of models were sold between October 1971 and January 1972; the Freeway is the best selling Dormobile model for this year; Dormobile announce that a 'Dormobile Register' will be set up to cater for the 40,000 Dormobile owners (their own figure); members will receive a quarterly newsletter, the opportunity to attend British meetings and special factory visits; Dormobile designer Cecil Carte died; he had joined Martin Walter Ltd in 1922 as an apprentice, becoming production manager by 1946, and was responsible for the design of the Dormatic seats; his final project was to head the design team working on the Bedford HA Roma; Dormobile announce a tax-exempt roof conversion for the Range Rover, now with a lined canopy, two bunks, lighting and curtains, all for £316.80; the company holds the first ever 'At Home' weekend in September on Folkestone Racecourse; this was for members of the Dormobile Owners Register and the cost was £3.50 per head; there is an exclusive factory visit to preview the 1973 model line-up.

1973 After the takeover of Dormobile by the Charringtons Group, David Tapley resigns; J.W. Sutton becomes managing director of Dormobile Ltd; Dormobile launch a new service to establish 200 motor caravan hire centres around the United Kingdom (for Dormobile campers); the Fiat Dormobile D4/8 is introduced to much acclaim.

1974 Dormobile expands its 'Special Facilities', when marketing director John Lambert announces that they will now add special features (such as external lockers) to motor caravans as specified by customers; the company launch a new campaign 'Refurbish Your Dormobile for Spring', offering to reupholster and retrim older models, the fitting of new curtains was also offered; Dormobile display a 'Pink Panther' special Freeway model at the Earls Court Motor Show, based on the Bedford CF; the vehicle features all-pink Dralon upholstery and curtains, together with an external pink colour scheme; also on display: the Ford Transit Freeway and the Bedford Land Cruiser with minor improvements; the Dormobile Coaster (Commer) and the Fiat Dormobile complete the show stand; new upholstery, designed for the aircraft industry, is now used on all Dormobile campers, with improved design, quality and fire retardant properties; the 'Highlander' is released by Dormobile, especially for the hire market; this an economy version of the Bedford CF Land Cruiser; the interior has room for two double beds, a single bunk over one of the doubles and a bunk in the driving cab for a small child; the British racing driver Tony Lanfranchi is loaned a Bedford CF Land Cruiser by Kents Motorcaravans, the vehicle is in his own racing livery of green; price rises to Dormobile models occur on 1 April because of the soaring cost of raw materials (according to Dormobile), the Freeway rises to £2,056, the Coaster to £1,890 and the Land Cruiser to £2,675; Sir John Trelawny leaves the board of Dormobile Ltd; an environmentally-friendly stainless steel silencer is now an option on the Bedford CF Land Cruiser.

1975 With a slump in British sales of motor caravans, Dormobile launch an economy camper van using an old name from the past, the Romany; this MkIII version, with basic facilities, was priced at £2,656+VAT.

1976 Early in the year Dormobile announce that they are willing to convert a customer's own VW van into a Dormobile D4/6 at a cost of £890+VAT.

1977 The Deauville coach-built motorhome makes its debut at the Caravan, Camping and Holiday Show held at Earls Court.

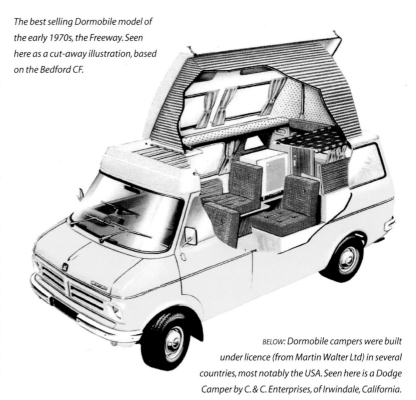

The best selling Dormobile model of the early 1970s, the Freeway. Seen here as a cut-away illustration, based on the Bedford CF.

BELOW: Dormobile campers were built under licence (from Martin Walter Ltd) in several countries, most notably the USA. Seen here is a Dodge Camper by C. & C. Enterprises, of Irwindale, California.

1982 By this year Dormobile have disappeared from the model/price listings in the monthly guides for motor caravans and are now listed only as offering a camper conversion on the Toyota.

1991 (31 May) *Kent News* reports that 180 jobs are in the balance at Dormobile, the coach-building firm having gone into receivership.

1991 (3 June) News reports indicate that sixty-two jobs are to go at Dormobile after it went into voluntary receivership.

1991 (26 July) Regional television in Kent reports that more jobs could be created at troubled engineering company Dormobile; a London firm had taken over the factory at Folkestone just days after 120 redundancies were announced; the new firm had pledged to take on as many ex-employees as possible and extend the range of specialist vehicles produced there.

1993 (27 November) Regional television in Kent carries news report about the fears for the future of 200 jobs at Dormobile and reveals that the company had been visited by High Court bailiffs who seized equipment; management were not available for comment.

1994 Final closure of the Folkestone factory, bringing to an end thirty-nine years of specialist vehicle building at the site.

2008 The site is now home to the Shearway Business Park.

During the course of my research I was able to speak to several people who worked for Martin Walter Ltd at the height of their popularity as motor caravan conversion specialists. They offered a fascinating insight to this once huge company, which for many years was one of the most prominent employers in the Folkestone area. One particular ex-employee by the name of Derick Boxall gave me a fascinating glimpse into the past. This is his story:

I started work at Martin Walters on the 3rd of January 1955 on a five-year apprenticeship; this was at their factory situated on Cheriton Road, Folkestone. On the first day I was shown around the factory, it was split up into several small workshops, with each one having its own foreman. He would be seated on a tall pedestal so that he could see everyone working. There was a strict 'no talking' policy in those days, and, if you were caught, the penalty was suspension from work for three days. I remember the trim shop being occupied only by women, and they made all the seat covers and headlining. In there was a lady by the name of Maud, a large person, she was the instigator of all the chaps being initiated with upholstery solution when they started work at the factory. This solution was poured all over you, and you had to let it dry.

I recall the busy machine shop where all the timber was cut, shaped and planed, with some going off to the steam shop and was used straight away as there was little storage room. Another machine shop would be where all the metal was cut, welded and bent to shape before going off to the paint shop. I remember the paint shop being split into two sections, one for dipping and galvanizing, and the other for paint spraying. There was also a huge glassfibre shop where all the camper van roofs were produced, and an additional shop for new products. There were also other large departments like the sub-assembly area for all the Dormobile interiors, and a jig and pattern shop with large technical drawings everywhere.

Another thing I recall were the fifty or so machinists on the ground floor, and a further twenty upstairs. A lot of the women were always putting the needles through their fingers, and, as a result, the first-aid hut was always a busy place. In this department all the fabric material came up on pallets; usually of the same colour for a month and then it was changed on a rota basis. Patterns of ply were laid on top of this material and cut with a large electric knife. Some of the upholsterers used to use tacks for fixing purposes, but I found this very dangerous when I spent some time working in there.

They would put a handful of tacks in their mouth, and then, with a magnetic hammer, they would flick the tack on to the hammer by using their tongue. I was alright doing this in small amounts but not large handfuls. Now and then someone would swallow a tack and that was hell when it happened. When I did it the nurse gave me a lump of cotton wool to swallow and you had to take the day off work, you can imagine the rest! It was painful for days, but apparently it did happen quite a lot.

Derick was just one of thousands of employees who worked at the Martin Walter factories over the years. As they were such a large employer in the area often whole families would be working at the factory in different departments, As the company had been established in the area for so long, it was one of those places where very often son would follow father and daughter would follow mother – a true several generational workplace. But today there is little or no evidence that the once great Martin Walter company ever existed, let alone Dormobile. It is quite sad when you consider that they were once the largest producer of specialist vehicles anywhere in the world. My sincere thanks to Derick and the others who have helped me to understand a little of what life was like making Dormobiles (and Utilicons, and Utilibrakes …).

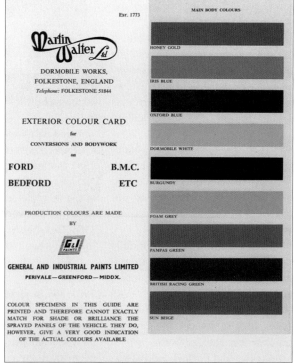

ABOVE: It certainly is not possible to save all Dormobiles, though it is fun to try. This Bedford Freeway looks to have been on its last holiday.
RIGHT: A Dormobile colour chart from the late 1960s (colours may vary slightly due to reproduction quality).

28

Dormobile caravans

ABOVE: Dormobile unveiled their touring caravan in 1969. Seen here is the economy 3.2 model being towed by a Triumph saloon car.

RIGHT: Constructed and awaiting the exterior paint finish in the Ashford factory.

BELOW RIGHT: Dormobile invested heavily in new equipment for the caravan factory at Ashford, Kent. Two employees are seen here fitting the joint sealing strips.

When a huge company such as Dormobile Ltd has such rich resources at its disposal by way of premises, specialist labour and an in-house design team, it is often necessary to diversify in order to make full use of them. Martin Walter Ltd had always done this over the years; examples included their stove enamelling section, which, as well as producing the metal cabinets for the Dormobile Land Rover model, was put to full use by producing other, much smaller stove-enamelled products not related to camping. Their huge fibreglass facility was also put to good use, again by manufacturing non-camping related items. Motor caravan and trailer caravan (tourer) construction have always shared similar build methods, and, of course, the internal materials within the 'living' area. A number of motor caravan converters began with caravan manufacture and later added, or switched to, camper van construction, for example Bluebird in the 1950s. Martin Walter Ltd had, at times during their long existence, built trailer caravans on a very small scale, but at the end of the 1960s they decided to enter this sector of the leisure industry with far greater determination than ever before.

In 1969 the announcement came of a new company being formed to produce Dormobile Trailer Caravans; the company name would be Dormobile Trailers (Ashford) Ltd, and it would be based at the former Martin Walter tyre sales depot on the Cobbs Industrial Estate at Ashford, Kent. This was a 15,000sq ft (1,400sq m) factory building, with plans to extend to 45,000sq ft (4,200sq m). The main figures at the newly formed company were Tom

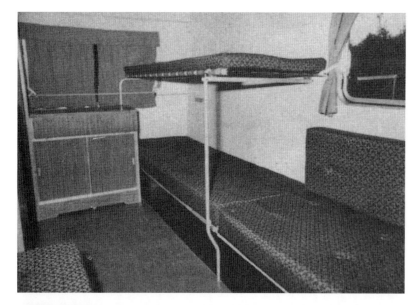

Sivyer, the marketing manager (recruited from a large caravan distributor in the south of England) and the works manager Roy Maxted, who had been involved with motor caravan production at Martin Walter Ltd for twenty-two years. The focal point of the new factory was a radio frequency thermo-bonding machine and this was used to glue the internal hardboard panels to the softwood frame in just seconds by using synthetic resins. This process of construction was not a new one, but few caravan manufacturers in the United Kingdom had one of these machines at the time.

Plans were set in place to appoint a Dormobile caravan distributor for every county in the country by the end of 1969, and to begin with Wilsons Motor Caravan Centre was appointed as the sole distributor for the Greater London area. But it was made clear that these caravans would not be available through the usual Dormobile camper van outlets, unless that company had an existing franchise for trailer caravans. Three Dormobile caravan models were released initially: the Dormobile 3.2 (a four-berth model), a two-berth De Luxe and also a larger Dormobile 4.2, which was a four-/five-berth caravan. The model designation numbers, the 3.2 and the 4.2, were, in fact, the length in metres of the caravans. All three models made their debut at the Caravan and Camping Show in 1969.

TOP: *Interior of the Dormobile 3.2 model. It was aimed at the economy end of the trailer caravan market. Note the use of tubular metal poles for the bunk bed support, an idea also used in the Land Cruiser camper vans.*

ABOVE: *An alternative view of the interior of the 3.2 model.*

RIGHT: *Model standards did improve with time and experience. Seen here is a more luxurious large caravan being exhibited at a caravan show.*

A Van For All Seasons

On fifty prototype models the company had used an aluminium exterior with a 'stucco' finish, but this idea was dropped due to difficulties in cleaning this rough surface. The company switched to the more traditional exterior painted finish; with this the aluminium was sprayed with an etching primer before a final coat of gloss paint developed by Glasso was applied. This was a particularly hard finish and was very resistant to scratches and light stone chips. Dormobile were using the popular 'Peak' chassis on which to construct their caravans, but did announce that they were in a position to produce their own chassis and might go down that route in the future. The fibreglass wheel arches on the caravans were produced in Folkestone.

These initial Dormobile caravans were no-nonsense, basic tourers with a low retail price; but they hardly took the British market by storm, which is best summed up by an extract from *The Caravan*, September 1969 after they had road-tested the new model:

Dormobile have been researching this move into trailers for some considerable time. The first announcement was made in 1968 and the first prototype appeared at the RAI Exhibition in Amsterdam earlier this year. With all this behind it, therefore it is something of an anticlimax that the new Dormobile [caravan] does not have more appeal. For a new maker to break into the market and aim at capturing a major share of it, he needs, however good his marketing techniques, a product that captures the imagination of the public and there is little about this van to do that. The van has many good points, not least its low price, and is a straightforward, no frills tourer.

The company obviously took on board these and similar comments on their new caravan, because as the 1970s unfolded they certainly did produce some far better models. The price of the Dormobile 3.2, four-berth caravan was £315 in the autumn of 1969, with the 3.2 De Luxe selling for £385 and the larger 4.2 for £440. It is also interesting to note that Dormobile produced a number of the popular trailer-tents from the same factory. The last known publicity I have been able to trace for Dormobile caravans is from the early 1980s, and, given the problems that Dormobile were experiencing at the time, it is possibly fair to assume that caravan production came to a halt around this date. Despite all those initial predictions about sales, possible exports and increased factory facilities, it does look as though the Dormobile caravan failed to make much of an impact on the caravan industry at the time, since several well-produced caravan histories published in recent years have failed to mention Dormobile caravans at all.

490C MODEL — 16' 1"
The 490C model has sleeping accommodation for four people with two extra long single beds or a giant double size bed at the rear end of the van and a normal size double bed at the front of the van — plus optional bunks if required. There is a spacious washroom/toilet compartment, full length wardrobe and centre kitchen.

420C MODEL — 13' 10"
The 420C model has sleeping accommodation for four people with a double bed at each end of the caravan — plus optional bunk beds if required. All models have the same spacious washroom/toilet compartment, full length wardrobe and centre kitchen.

370C MODEL — 12' 1"
The 370C model has a spacious washroom/toilet compartment and comfortable sleeping accommodation for three people with double bed at rear end and a single bed at the front — plus optional bunk beds if required. There is a full length wardrobe with shelf space and a well planned kitchen sink unit.

A trio of Dormobile tourers, on the left the 490C, the 420C in the centre and the 370C on the far right.

The author enjoys his first motorcaravan foray in the late 1960s. The vehicle is a home-converted BMC LD ambulance.

further reading

H. Myhill, *Motor Caravanning*
(Ward Locke Ltd, 1976)
Written by the long-time motor-caravanner and author Henry Myhill (who, incidentally, lived in a Bluebird Highwayman for several years). Although intended as a guide for motor caravanners, it is now of interest to classic camper enthusiasts simply because of the models mentioned and the accompanying photographs.

T. Wilkinson, *Motor Caravanning*
(David & Charles, 1968)
This book contains some interesting model profiles, line drawings and excellent photographs. Written as a guide for the period, it now represents a good reference guide for classic followers.

S. Lyons, *Motorcaravanning at Home and Abroad*
(Yeoman Publications, 1973)
This book is really more of a 'how to' publication. It contains few photographs and instead relies on cartoon drawings by 'Nardi' of humorous camping moments.

W.M. Whiteman, *The History of the Caravan*
(Blandford Press, 1973)
Highly regarded as one of the best books written on caravanning history. Whiteman was the founder of the Caravan Council in 1939 and editor of *Caravan* for twenty-two years. This book, as the title suggests, is mainly concerned with touring/trailer caravans, but does also have a section about camper vans and includes two pictures of early Dormobile models. An interesting read for anyone with an interest in British caravans and their development.

J. Hunt, *The Practical Motorcaravanner*
(David & Charles, 1983)
Written by John Hunt, one of the most respected motor caravan journalists in the United Kingdom. Hunt introduced the first monthly magazine for motor-caravanners, which went on sale to the public in 1966. Many models were altered by the conversion company after Hunt had road-tested the prototypes and pointed out their shortcomings. This book is a guide to motor-caravanning and makes reference to many of the models and base vehicles of the classic period.

C. Park, *The Complete Book of Motorcaravanning*
(Haynes, 1979)
An excellent, large format book, which, because of its publication date, is especially interesting to classic camper enthusiasts. Yet another guide to motor-caravanning, packed with photographs of the classic models.

N. Wilson, *Gypsies and Gentlemen*
(Columbus Books, 1986)
Not of great interest to classic enthusiasts, but a fascinating work for anyone interested in the development of caravanning, camping and motor-caravanning. A very good historical book tracing the camping culture from early horse-drawn wagons through to F/M Viscount Montgomery's motorhomes, which he used during the Second World War.

J. Hanson, *The Story of the Motor Caravan*
(Malvern House Publications, 1997)
The smallest of all the books mentioned here, this was produced in A5 format in the style of a booklet. The northern-based transport historian John Hanson is a dedicated enthusiast of vintage, veteran and classic motor caravans and owns several himself. Although small in size, the book contains many excellent photographs, a large proportion of which were published here for the first time.

D. Eccles, *VW Camper: The Inside Story*
(The Crowood Press, 2005)
Highly regarded as one of the best books of its type by both VW camper fanatics and motoring historians. For my part, I believe it to be the best book available, detailing nearly every model of VW camper between 1951 and 2005. No Volkswagen camper owner, enthusiast or fan can afford not to have this.

K. Trant, *Home Away from Home*
(Black Dog Publishing, 2006)
Despite being the largest book of all those discussed here, this is a curious publication as it does not easily fall into any specific category. It is certainly not a guidebook, but more of a reference work, taking a look at owners and their campers, both in the United Kingdom and the USA. Although aimed heavily at the American market, it does include many British owners describing their campers and why they enjoy using them.

M. Watts, *Classic Camper Vans: The Inside Story*
(The Crowood Press, 2007)
This book takes an in-depth look at all the most popular British camper vans built between 1956 and 1979. It covers the history of camper vans in the United Kingdom and includes a full summary of events in the industry in that period. It uses a good mixture of pictures through which to illustrate the models and includes many period brochure covers and advertisements. It also has a section featuring some weird and wonderful camper van models. A must-have book for any classic camper van owner or enthusiast.

owners' clubs & useful contacts

Because Dormobile camper vans were produced for so long and in huge numbers, it is understandable that large numbers of them have survived, even from the early days of production (give or take a couple of examples). No classic vehicle show or large steam rally in the United Kingdom would be complete without a couple of Dormobile camper vans being present. When it comes to surviving Dormobile campers, their owners have a good choice of clubs from which to choose, if they want to feel part of a wider community of like-minded enthusiasts. Many, of course, face something of a dilemma, because Dormobile used such a varied number of chassis over the years, and so often the owner has the option of joining a specialist club catering for his particular chassis, such as Bedford, or a more general club for all older camper vans.

There are a number of owners' clubs in Britain and further afield that accept the base vehicle into their ranks, irrespective of the fact that it may be a camper van, and there are also a number of specialized clubs such as the Standard Motor Club (Atlas), the J2 Register (Austin 152 and Morris J2) and the Ford 400E Owners' Club (Ford Thames). On the other hand, owners have the choice of joining a more general club for older camper vans, such as the Classic Camper Club or the Period Motorcaravan Guild. There is certainly no shortage of groups, clubs and associations for owners of Dormobile camper models, and there are also many internet forums that offer help and assistance; some of these have a joining fee and some do not.

In this section I have listed as many of these clubs, groups and associations as I could. By their very nature, these clubs do have a change of officials from time to time and so, although the details published were correct at the time of writing, it would make sense to check details via an internet search engine or by purchasing an up-to-date copy of a classic car or motor caravan magazine. At the end of this club/forum listing I have added a further reference section that relates to 'Dormobile specific parts', such as replacement roof seals and roof vents, giving contact details of suppliers able to assist present day owners.

OWNERS' CLUBS

Classic Camper Club
(*all campers up to 1987*)
30 Fairwater Crescent, Alcester,
Warwickshire B49 6RB;
www.classiccamperclub.co.uk

Dormobile Owners Club
(*all genuine Dormobile campers*)
Secretary, 67 Upper Shelton Road,
Marston Moretaine, Bedfordshire
MK43 0LU; www.dormobile.org.uk

Ford 400E Owners Club
(**Ford Thames 400E**)
Sandy Glen, 1 Maltings Cottage,
Witham Road, White Notley, Witham,
Essex CM8 1SE

Land Rover Series 2 Club
(*all Land Rover Series 2-based
Dormobiles*)
PO Box 61, Aberdaire CF44 4AJ;
www.series2club.co.uk

Period Motorcaravan Guild
(*all Dormobile camper vans up to
1972*)
John Hanson, 116 Copgrove Road,
Leeds LS8 2RS;
www.brmmbrmm.com/periodmcg

Split Screen Van Club
(*all VW split screen models*)
Welbeck House, Manor Road, Burgess
Hill, Sussex RH16 0NW;
www.ssvc.org.uk

Standard Motor Club
(*Standard cars and commercials*)
Secretary: Rachel Maxwell, 5
Woodcroft Close, Highfields, Towcester,
Northants NN12 6DB;
www.standardmotorclub.org.uk

VW Type 2 Owners Club
(*VW Dormobile D4/6 and D4/8*)
57 Humphrey Avenue, Bromsgrove,
Worcestershire B60 3JD;
www.vwt2oc.com

INTERNET FORUMS
(*suited to Dormobile camper vans*)

www.bedford-cf.co.uk
(*all things Bedford CF-related*)
www.bedford-world.com
(*all Bedford commercials*)
www.commervanfan.co.uk
(*Commer/Dodge Spacevan*)
www.fordtransit.org/forum
(*history and forum*)
www.transitvanclub.co.uk
(*history, gallery and events*)
www.classiccamperclub.co.uk
(*follow links*)

DORMOBILE PARTS SUPPLIERS

Atlantis Classics
The Old School, Silver Street, Whitwick,
Coalville, Leicestershire LE67 5EW;
www.atlantisclasics.co.uk
(*sells new vehicle badges, including
Dormobile metal badges*)

Dormobile Ltd
Premier Way, Abbey Park Industrial
Estate, Romsey, Hants SO51 9DQ;
www.dormobile.co.uk
(*supplier of parts for the Dormobile Land
Rover; also sells new parts to convert the
Land Rover 110 and 109, including the
Dormobile roof; will also convert the
Land Rover Dormobile to order*)

Individual Interiors (Camper Shop)
The Old Post Office, Upton upon
Severn, Worcestershire WR8 0QL;
www.campershop.co.uk
(*supplier of many items required to
renovate/restore a Dormobile rising roof,
including new roof bellows (fabric),
rubber seals, plastic roof vents, roof
toggle catches and hinges*)

Just Kampers
Unit 1, Stapley Manor, Long Lane,
Odiham, Hampshire RG29 1JT;
www.justkampers.com
(*supplier of numerous mechanical parts
for all Volkswagen Transporters; supplies
several replacement parts required for
renovating, including the Dormobile roof*)

Status VW Parts
Unit 2C, Old Station Road, Kirkby
Lonsdale LA6 2HP;
www.status-vw.co.uk
(*supplier of several parts required to
renovate a Dormobile roof, including
new roof seals, vent seals and roof
window seals*)

index